ANTIPOLITICS

Critical Acclaim for *Antipolitics*

"Laced with wit and informed by a patriotism that is intense without being arrogant or exclusive. His vision of the desirable and the possible speaks for—and to—hope all over the world."

— *The New Yorker*

"Konrád offers 'Antipolitics' as the moral surveillance and supervision required to confine politics to its proper limits...[his] prescription is tempered by the experience and pragmatism of a spirited conscience."

— *Boston Herald*

"Refreshing and rewarding...In conditions more conducive to pessimism and one-sided judgments than ours, he has produced a resounding assertion of political optimism and critical balance."

— *New Statesman*

"A militant call for ideological disarmament and a complex argument in favor of simple decency."

— *The Boston Globe*

"An excellent insight."

— *Library Journal*

"A courageous and provocative rallying cry."

— *Publishers Weekly*

ANTIPOLITICS

GEORGE KONRÁD

AN ESSAY

Translated from the Hungarian by Richard E. Allen

An Owl Book

Henry Holt and Company
NEW YORK

Published by Henry Holt and Company, Inc.,
521 Fifth Avenue, New York, New York 10175.
Distributed in Canada by Fitzhenry & Whiteside Limited,
195 Allstate Parkway, Markham, Ontario L3R 4T8.

Library of Congress Cataloging-in-Publication Data
Konrád, György.
Antipolitics: an essay.
"An Owl book."
1. Europe—Politics and government—1945-
2. Europe—Foreign relations—1945-   . 3. United
States—Foreign relations—Soviet Union. 4. Soviet Union
—Foreign relations—United States. I. Title.
[D1058.K597 1987]   909.82′8   87–192
ISBN 0-8050-0357-6 (pbk.)

First published in hardcover by Harcourt Brace Jovanovich, Inc.
in 1984.
First Owl Book Edition—1987
Printed in the United States of America
10 9 8 7 6 5 4 3 2 1

ISBN 0-8050-0357-6

ANTIPOLITICS

Peace: Anti-Yalta

To find the main reason for today's threat of war, we must go back to the year 1945, to Yalta. It was there that a helpless Europe was divided; it was there that agreements were reached for military zones of occupation that would become political spheres of interest as well. Yalta gave birth to a system of international relations based upon a state of rivalry and equilibrium between the Soviet Union and the United States. Whether the three old gentlemen who met there knew it or not, the idea of the Iron Curtain was born at Yalta, a symbol of great-power logic. Three old men—Roosevelt, Stalin, and Churchill—decided the fate of hundreds of millions for decades to come, the hundreds of millions having to respect their decision.

What a dirty trick of history! The allies who were defending mankind from fascist inhumanity hastened, on the very eve of victory, to strike an imperialist bargain, a pact between Anglo-Saxon and Soviet imperialism. They were able to do it because they commanded the biggest battalions, and went ahead and did it because—despite all the universalist rhetoric—nationalism, the ideology of the expansive nation-state, impelled them to. They thought it their historic right as victors to dictate the terms of peace. They made the mistake of thinking—whether in good faith or bad, we don't know—that on the will of the victor can be based the peace of a continent. A mistake with a long history, to be sure: for thousands of years, an unjust peace following one war has led to the next conflict. A powerful victor makes an arbitrary peace that the vanquished cannot accept.

The implication of Yalta is that the military status quo determines the political status quo. The morality of Yalta is simple: those who have the bombs and tanks decide the social and political system. Since the United States and the Soviet Union had the most bombs and tanks, they were called to lead the world. Later—by the fearful light of Hiroshima—their calling was confirmed, for only these two giant nation-states had the resources to build arsenals of nuclear weapons.

Thus whoever has the power of annihilation is called to lead the world. The Soviet and American presidents have more power than all the tyrants of history combined. Jehovah had power because he could destroy the world. I look at those two faces and I blanch. I wouldn't entrust the fate of humanity to even Aristotle and Kant. Is it possible that the destiny of mankind will be a parody? Is it possible that the Lord means to put an end to our species through a second Fall? Did He put the button of the Last Judgment under the fingers of two vain, frail old men? If they are human, like all the sons and daughters of Cain, their fingers must weigh heavily on the button. I don't trust in their wisdom, only in their fear of death.

The present status quo in Europe represents the petrifaction of an exceptional state of postwar occupation. Diplomatic declarations and the political consensus of nations agree in presenting this exceptional situation as a normal state of affairs. At Helsinki all the states involved solemnly declared that henceforward this absurdity would be law.

Why does the West refuse to accept the presence of Soviet troops in Afghanistan? Because they haven't been there very long. Their presence in East Central Europe is reasonable and acceptable by now, because they have been there nearly forty years. And it is all the more acceptable because American forces are present in Western Europe.

Limited national sovereignty, as circumscribed by the terms of the Warsaw Pact, is bearable because the rather more loosely restricted national sovereignty defined by NATO is bearable. Indeed, both sets of limitations are geopolitical givens, respected by every rational politician. To question the partition of Europe is dangerous and misleading, because it fosters the illusion that it is possible to question it.

The West is not strong enough to compel the Soviet forces stationed in other countries to return home. At most, it can protest their expansion, however little impact that may make on Soviet military conduct. If, however, the West really wants to see those forces return home, why not make the Russians an offer advantageous to both sides? One might, for example, propose a mutual and balanced withdrawal of forces—not reduction, but withdrawal. Is it a mad fancy to enunciate the principle that no country should keep soldiers on the territory of another? I remember how, on October 23, 1956, the young men and women of Budapest chanted their new rhyme:

Soldiers from everywhere,
Go home and stay there.

I have liked this little verse ever since; a quarter of a century later, it seems more timely than ever.

A hard rule to follow, granted! There are always reasons for offering hospitality to foreign troops. A great power easily finds cooperative local politicians who will call in its forces, set up a client government, and then legalize the presence of the great power's troops, claiming it is the will of the occupied nation. There is always some mounting danger to avert, of course, always something sacred to defend—humanitarian interests, revolutionary achievements, democratic principles; the people's welfare must be defended from the people themselves.

I don't know of a single instance where one of the great powers occupied a small country in order to topple a local dictatorship and thereby free the people. If it is only a matter of a tyrannical regime oppressing a people, then—regrettably—national sovereignty must be respected and interference in internal affairs avoided. Idi Amin's grotesque depredations were tolerated by both great powers. They both have their share of client dictatorships, picturesque and absurd, but no one will trouble these petty dictators as long as they don't go against the interests of their patrons.

The interests of the great powers, and theirs alone, demand that they keep troops on the soil of other countries. The United States keeps 350,000 soldiers as a tripwire in Europe; it has accepted responsibility for West Berlin; in what is increasingly a symbolic gesture, it maintains conventional forces in Western Europe, on a soil that more and more is shifting beneath their feet. The ground is shaky beneath the Russians' feet, too, simply because they are here in Europe and not at home in the Soviet Union. Eastern Europe's nationalisms have reawakened, and it will be more and more difficult to put them to sleep again.

What is needed is not so much a radical change in the relations of military power as some way for normal social, economic, and cultural conditions to assert themselves freely and fully. It is not at all certain that the two superpowers must come to blows. Let them go on demonstrating that they can spend ever increasing sums on sophisticated weaponry; they will not gain much by it.

At the present time no one has a comprehensive strategy for peace. There is no theory about how the present system of international relations might be transformed. Neither West nor East has been able to make a broad, historic proposal to the other. No recommendations have appeared on positive ways to bring about coexistence and greater partnership. Only broad proposals are worth making, since partial ones invariably founder amid mutual suspicion. It is worthwhile thinking only in terms of the alternatives of war and peace, not in terms of the ebb and flow of détente and the Cold War.

It might seem easier for the West, which is less inflexible, to offer a useful alternative proposal to tame the bear. It is remarkable that the West, with its knack for achieving sensible compromises, has as yet made no concrete and comprehensive proposal to the Soviet Union. Not only has no government done so; no Western society has offered a rational plan which would carry advantages for the power elite and hence be acceptable to them, which would afford some scope in the world to the Russian people's pride, and which would not link peace to the humiliation of the Russian elite. The world is big enough for their abilities to find a place in it, too.

It is possible to imagine the gradual, controlled transformation of the Soviet empire—the U.S.S.R. and its dependent allies—into a community of nations capable of behaving like a partner toward the countries of Western Europe. Such a development, while making greater demands on the intelligence of the Soviet intellectual community, would also assure them of more initiative in world affairs. Today that is not the case: there are more Soviet agents in the world than scholars and students. The Russians must be afforded tranquillity so they can reform their economy and administrative system. They must have help if they are to put their fear of attack behind them and turn their faces toward the West. For if the Soviet Union doesn't want war, it must accept the pluralism which spans the northern hemisphere from Europe to America and on to Japan (and which may one day continue on across China and Russia to complete the circle).

To date the West has had no positive strategy of peace; it has merely rejected with suspicion the more or less propagandistic proposals of the Soviets. But the West doesn't lack the political capacity to take a creative initiative. Standing by Yalta is not a long-term strategy, but merely a ratification of the status quo, which is an impossibility in any longer perspective. The peoples of Central Europe should ponder this carefully; twice already, unsettled conditions in their region have led to world war.

If the West wants Yalta, the Soviet Union will move beyond Yalta—by moving westward. If the West wants Yalta, it can have November 4, 1956, in Budapest, August 21, 1968, in Prague, and December 13, 1981, in Warsaw. After every such aggression the West laments, protests, and looks on with alarm. Then by and by it signs a new agreement, largely for public relations purposes, while in the background the arms race goes on undisturbed.

The Americans and the Russians both demonstrate what they can do. The more they demonstrate it, the more threatened they feel. Disarmament has never yet been mutual, and so it has never been successful. Technical agreements about the size of arsenals don't lead to peace. It is difficult to dissuade any leadership from arming, if it feels threatened.

The Soviet Union has less room for maneuver because the tensions are building up within its empire; yet the leaders want to maintain that empire because they identify the empire's survival with their own. Anxious about their own power, they try to reassure themselves by overarming. As long as they will not negotiate about a German peace treaty and reunification, their troops will remain in Hungary and missiles will be pointed at Hungarian cities.

The present situation is unnatural and unsettling. The Iron Curtain gives rise to fears on both sides that the other will try to breach it, and provokes efforts by both sides to prevent that through military superiority. We have every reason to demand a general settlement; addressing the great questions of the day should not wait upon petty party squabbles. Deciding how to maintain the military balance following a mutual troop withdrawal would be a technical matter. Before that, however, political agreement must be reached on the questions that can profitably be taken up. So long as Russian and American troops glare at each other across the Elbe, there must be a better alternative. But what is it?

A United States of Europe based on the transcendence of a common European undertaking is the only possibility. A United States of *Western* Europe simply won't work in the present political context, since some Western European states belong to the Atlantic alliance while others have chosen neutrality. And Western European unity is being eroded still further by the divisive ideological struggles that surface as more and more Western Europeans, faced with a bipolar world, are drawn to neutrality. Today's Western Europe has no independent political philosophy, and so it offers none of the transcendence that would give meaning to a common enterprise like integration.

America perhaps refuses to concert its strategy with its European allies because the allies have no consistent strategy. Those allies want to preserve the status quo, but events are running ahead of them. There are independent national policies; these differ from the overall Atlantic course, however, less as creative initiatives than in their greater indulgence toward the Soviet bloc.

Not a single European government has made the cardinal peace proposal: an appeal for the removal of the Iron Curtain. Europe's politicians have no bold, incisive peace strategy and don't seek to launch any useful debate. This intellectual passivity is simply a retreat before Soviet peace propaganda, which uses military force to make Europeans and the whole world acknowledge that what the Soviets acquired in World War II is theirs. From the Pacific Ocean to the Iron Curtain, their empire is a seamless whole; to contest it from within is counterrevolution, while to contest it from without is to meddle in their internal affairs. The Helsinki Declaration only confirmed, three decades afterward, the validity of the agreements reached at Yalta and, later in 1945, at Potsdam.

It is pleasant to commiserate with the unfortunate Eastern European cousins, but let no one think the West is going to make any trouble on their account. They got détente, they got credits, what more do they want? What more? They want a creative initiative, a concrete, tangible peace proposal, a plan to take down the Iron Curtain. They want Western Europeans to understand that while Eastern Europe remains under occupation, Western Europeans cannot live in security. Western Europe is moving toward neutrality of its own accord, without even trying to demand that Eastern Europe be neutralized in exchange. It takes little intelligence to cling to the ideology either of blind loyalty to NATO or of unilateral concessions. Western Europe will find a worthy place for itself in the world only when it no longer allows the U.S.-Soviet dichotomy to determine its place.

To prevent a third world war, all foreign troops must be withdrawn from Europe. The fundamental guarantee of peace is a mutual agreement among the European states to withdraw from the two military blocs and abolish the Iron Curtain. Through a process of gradual integration, the western corner of the Eurasian land mass might then develop into a European confederation.

Does it make sense to ask whether there are any proposals for a nonviolent solution that might prevent Europe from becoming the scene of a third and final world war? It is we who are at stake, we Europeans. It is because of us that the two greatest nation-states in the world confront each other. Our intellectual failings brought about the baleful situation in which our continent is cut in two. European nation-states, European political doctrines, and the collective short-sightedness of respected European politicians are responsible for the Iron Curtain. No European political class is blameless; no European nation is exempt. Nowhere in Europe can a realistic public opinion pretend that it remains unaffected by the Iron Curtain, by its influence today and its possible consequences tomorrow.

It is an unobservant European who fails to notice that the Iron Curtain is made of explosive material. Western Europe rests its back against a wall of dynamite, while blithely gazing out over the Atlantic. I consider Western Europe's good fortune as uncertain as our misfortune. Caught between the United States and the Soviet Union, we Europeans can assure peace only if we detach ourselves from them militarily by mutual agreement, and then go on to draw the two parts of a divided Europe together again.

THE INTERNATIONAL IDEOLOGICAL WAR:
A CONTEST OF NATIONAL POLITICAL ELITES

If we were to consider carefully, as a student of contemporary history might, what concrete conflicts of interest divide the Soviet and American people today, we would be surprised to find how few there are. And if we looked to see how many opportunities for mutually beneficial cooperation between the two there are, if they suspended the ideological war, we would be surprised at how many there are.

The ideological war is a fact, but far from an unalterable fact. It is the only war against which ideas have a chance of success, of building bridges between Moscow and Washington. It is precisely this hope that should spur independent people everywhere to apply the closest ethical scrutiny to those intellectuals who, under the Damocles' sword of multiple overkill, go on pursuing the intellectually sterile operations of ideological war, fraying the slender cord by which the sword is suspended. Intellectual cheerleaders are more dangerous today than ever before.

Ideology is a cloud that obscures as much as it explains; it confers upon the world whatever shape we like. Ideological competition follows from the existence of ideologies, but it doesn't follow that the competition must also be a nuclear one. It follows from the nature of ideology that our age has a certain style. More and more, the style of our time is to treat our human situation as a game—a game with ever more precise rules. It is an immanent, relativistic, understanding approach, dialectical, ironic, and critical of ideology. Part of this game is to subject to close intellectual and moral scrutiny those feverish laborers in the vineyard of ideological war as they pursue, with staggering conscientiousness, their labors of obfuscation.

In point of fact, it is not ideologies that contend today, nor is it systems like capitalism and communism. Anyone who believes that two systems and two ideologies are pitted against each other today has fallen victim to the secularized metaphysics of our civilization, which looks for a duel between God and Satan in what is, after all, only a game. Russians and Americans—their political classes, that is— circle each other in the ring. Each of the two world heavyweight champions would like to show he is the strongest in the world; they are playing a game with each other whose paraphernalia include nuclear missiles. Yet it is impossible to construct from the Soviet-American conflict an ideological dichotomy along whose axis the values of our continent can be ranged. The antitheses which fill our mental horizon —capitalism versus state socialism, democracy versus totalitarianism, market economy versus planned economy—are forced mythologies which the intelligentsias of East and West either confuse with reality or else, being aware that they are not very precise appellations, seek to square with the real facts.

What is basic and decisive is the strategy of the nation-state, which the political class of every nation devises and then declares to be identical with their country's interest. The various universalist appeals to the working class or to Christianity, to freedom or to socialism, are merely weapons in the strategy of the nation-state. We stand close to a third world war today because the American and Russian political classes have chosen a strategy of confrontation and of a prestige fight for world supremacy.

Politicians do the things they do because they want to do them, and for no other reason. If they didn't want to do them, they wouldn't. They would step down and cease to be politicians. If politicians make war, then the war has happened because the politicians wanted to make war. We too are at fault when these men take us into war, because, from stupidity or cowardice, we let them play with fire. I consider the demythologizing of politics to be the first duty of grown, thinking people. It is our business because it is the only way we can save our lives.

Europe suffered two world wars because of Franco-German rivalry, which once appeared so fateful but today seems quite contrived. The question of who should be master in Europe played a larger role in their contest than any concrete economic, demographic, or territorial conflict of interest. The game ended both times with the far-from-glorious triumph of France, and along the way Europe fell under the domination of the two peripheral powers, the Soviet Union and the United States. The question was answered: the strongest nation in Europe (or Eurasia) was neither France nor Germany, but Russia.

Ideologies played their part, too, but the struggle of nations was the essential thing, and the result was what might have been expected: the biggest nation was the strongest one. A race for prestige between two middle-sized European nations delivered up our continent to two enormous extra-European nation-states. Neither ideology nor any continental community of interest was able to prevent the struggle of the political classes of those two states for the hegemony of Europe. If there had been no Franco-German rivalry, there would have been no World War I; if there had been no World War I, there would have been no Hitler. If there had been no Hitler, there would have been no Yalta.

Yet all of European culture bore responsibility for World War I, philosophies as well as historical theories, poetic myths as well as formulations of interest. The fundamental values of the European intelligentsia were to blame as well as the bluster of the nation-state.

All three universal spiritual currents—Christianity, liberalism, and socialism—subordinated themselves to the ethos of particularism, the sentimental belligerence of the nation-state's bureaucracy—nationalism. Army chaplains rendered abundantly unto Caesar the things that were his; they exalted the murderous heroic deed. Liberals, according to their nineteenth-century custom, identified the conquest or defense of markets and sources of raw materials with the defense of civilization. Socialists looked into their hearts and discovered that they were no worse patriots than the others; they too could shoot at their comrades of other nationalities. From Zurich, meanwhile, Lenin saw that war economy offered a royal road to a system of redistributive state communism.

The romanticism of the nation-state triumphed everywhere. Overrefined poets prattled of redemption by fire;

impotence identified vigor with bloodshed. And what has happened since? Nothing. Another world war, with three times as many dead, then the preparation of the physical and spiritual arsenal for a third. And the cream of our culture is complicitous in that labor of preparation, by virtue of their feckless impotence in the face of it.

It was totally senseless that so many people should perish over the foolish question of who should rule in Europe—Germans or Frenchmen—for the question was answerable in advance: neither would rule. Nor was it a novel notion even then that each and every people should take care of its own affairs, cooperating with the others in linking together the cultures and institutions of the continent to create a better society.

Today too, it is completely senseless for us to die over the foolish question of who is to rule the world—Russia or America. Neither is going to rule. Neither has a right or a mission to lead the world, nor indeed even the potential to do so. To be sure, both superpowers have an interest in justifying their egotism by appealing to some universal, international, and majoritarian principle of legitimacy. A powerful nation-state can found its claims to quasi-global authority only on supranational values in the second half of the twentieth century, following the collapse of the German bid for world hegemony with its heavy reliance on nationalistic ideas. For world dominion, universalist ideas are required today; and the real interests of the inhabitants of every country must be linked with those ideas.

The driving force behind the struggle for world power is not an ideological commitment to any social and political system, or to the values of a given culture; it is the craving of the strongest national elites for world dominion as found primarily in their political class, and in their military and technical elites as well. It is likely that the representatives of both the Russian and American power elite fancy the idea that they have a mission to lead the world. Men can invent few libidinous fantasies more enjoyable than those of world domination. For the power professional, power on a world-wide scale is the greatest earthly good.

The alternatives to the ideal of world power can only be metaphysical, ethical, aesthetic, and scientific; but states-men, by reason of their occupation, are necessarily more interested in political power than in metaphysics or ethics, aesthetics or scientific knowledge. The medium of politics is power over people—power backed up by weapons. The not very cultivated intelligentsia that forms the political, mili-tary, and bureaucratic elite of every nation-state is too red-blooded and too commonplace to find any pleasure more voluptuous than the sensual experience of power.

ADVOCATE OF HUMAN RIGHTS:
WHICH SUPERPOWER?

The Russians say that their conflict with America is a class struggle, that the contest of nation-states has a class charac-ter in which they represent the international working class, and America the international bourgeoisie. Yet an American worker might well wonder what advantages the Russian workers have that need to be defended, by force of arms if necessary. The working class holds power in neither America nor Russia, and by whatever name one characterizes the power elites of these two great states, no workers are to be found in their ranks.

In the one country as in the other it is politicians, high-level bureaucrats, industrial and military leaders, influential experts and ideologues, diplomats, and leading academics who are in the saddle. No doubt there are differences between the two countries in the composition of their power elites, but they are not great enough to explain in sociological terms the present nuclear confrontation.

Unquestionably, these two elites are engaged in an international competition. We would like, however, to narrow the circle of competitors somewhat. It is not at all certain that the top-level managers of the Russian and American economies feel that they are involved in a life-and-death struggle with each other. They can find as many reasons for cooperation as for conflict. Nor do I see any reason why there shouldn't be room on earth for Russia's writers, artists, and scholars and for their American counterparts as well. Even Russian and American boxers, it seems to me, have little desire to aim nuclear missiles at each other, tough customers though they undoubtedly are.

In the Soviet world, Marxism-Leninism provides an explanation for the missiles: the irreconcilable, unrelenting struggle between bourgeoisie and proletariat, between the capitalist and socialist world systems. Peaceful coexistence is only an ideological concession, justified as a more effective form of international class struggle that demands less sacrifice of human life. It's even possible to manipulate the clichés of Marxist-Leninist literature in such a way that nuclear missiles follow from peaceful coexistence itself.

On the Russian side the conflict is the work of politicians, military men, ideologues, and journalists, while the rest of society, bewildered and beguiled by propaganda, has little choice but to go along, though many certainly believe that the imperialists seriously threaten them and that America is the source of the biggest trouble. However rapidly Russian national sentiment and a neo-Slavophile sense of mission may be gaining ground in their society, the Russian political elite still need Marxism-Leninism, if only because it holds together their empire and assures them supporters elsewhere in the world.

Why should other nations be enthusiastic about the Russians being the dominant nation in Europe, or even indeed in the world? The expansionist rhetoric of one nation is not enough to assure the integrity of a multinational empire. Russophilism may be useful to make Russian hearts swell with pride; for the Ukrainians, Estonians, and Tadzhiks, however, a Soviet ideology is needed. Yet it is no secret in Kiev and Tbilisi, I think, that this ideology comes labeled "Made in Moscow." It is the ideology of Russian domination.

For those outside the Soviet Union, something else is required: the ideology of the world socialist movement, in which belonging to the Soviet camp is a source of pride and not misfortune.

Here in Budapest it's perfectly clear that Marxism-Leninism is needed to explain why Soviet troops are still here, almost forty years after the end of World War II. The legitimacy of Marxism-Leninism is reinforced also by feelings of respect for the hundreds of thousands of Russian soldiers who fell on Hungarian, Polish, and Czech soil during World War II. Even today their sacrifice is often emphasized in the private conversation of Soviet leaders to explain why they regard our western (rather than our eastern) borders as their own frontier. The Soviet dead and the socialist world system are reason enough why we should go on living the way we do and not the way that would be proper and natural for us.

What is at stake are Russian interests, but the Russians act as if it were the interests of socialism. And they are wise to do so: the fascist experiments demonstrated that radical nationalism, with its mythology of an exclusive ruling nation, can never offer a permanent basis for dominion over other peoples. Soviet Marxism, on the other hand, is an export commodity. There is a demand for it in the developing countries, where it may come in handy for those destined to be the intellectuals, military leaders, and officials of the local dictatorships, and where it may be needed as a source of hope by the workers who toil on the periphery of the capitalist world, where there is neither consumer abundance nor democracy. And of course Marxism-Leninism has its followers, loyal to Moscow, beyond the confines of the Soviet bloc. Their relationship to the Soviet Union can be complex and indirect, but for the most part it is direct enough and not very complicated.

First comes Soviet Marxism, then come arms exports, advisers to help introduce the Soviet model, organizational experience with secret police and state culture. State-social-ist dictatorship may not be perfect, but it offers a simple working model and is at least as exportable as liberal market economy and pluralist democracy. State society can be created quickly, but civil society takes a long time to build. Martial law can be proclaimed within hours. In one day, a whole host of things can be forbidden. One can nationalize easily, quickly, and decisively. The know-how and tech-nology are ready at hand; the advisers know exactly how to apply them. It would be ungracious to expect them to know how to assure the freedom and well-being of a country as well.

It would be all the more ungracious because the Ameri-cans don't dispatch experts on freedom and well-being to the Third World either. To their Central American neigh-bors they send the same goods as the Russians, it seems: weapons and police experts. There are and will be pro-Soviet societies in the Third World to whom America can offer no better alternative than competition on the open world market—a competition in which those societies, unless unusually rich in natural resources, have a very small chance of coming out ahead.

In Vietnam, America suffered a sociological, cultural, and ideological defeat even before the failure of its military effort. It proved unable to offer South Vietnam any sort of reform outweighing the lure of communism. Since then, it appears, the American elite has learned little from its de-feat. However prodigally it may give out money for weap-ons, it is as parsimonious as ever with the world's poor countries when it comes to giving out knowledge and democratic rights.

Like the Soviet Union in Eastern Europe, the United States cannot make itself loved in Latin America. In both places, crude national interest and great-power arrogance show through only too clearly. Nationalism in Eastern Europe is anti-Soviet, and in Latin America anti-American. The arrogance of power so blinds the Soviet and American elites that they can only take offense at this without being able to do anything about it. They are incapable of dealing with small nations in the way they should and the way those nations expect: on a footing of equality.

For Vietnam, things were different after the whole of that country came within the Soviet sphere of influence. The millennium did not dawn then and there for Vietnam, and the Vietnamese had to learn that the world they had fought for was a hard, hard world indeed. Little by little, the small nations are learning that it is not well to pay homage to either great power, and that the enemy of one's enemy is far from being one's friend. This accumulating experience may very well set bounds to the spread of Soviet Marxism and the Soviet model. The markets know the merchandise now, and the demand for it is falling off. The Great Russian exporter has to find a fresh packaging and a new marketing strategy.

It has been even easier for the American elite to cloak an itch for world power in the form of an ethic of global responsibility, in part perhaps because the Americans remained isolationist for so long, well past the time when their Russian counterparts had become frank expansionists. The American elite has a global responsibility to democracy and perhaps even to God as well. God and democracy: there you have America's Marxism-Leninism. And if, in the defense of those two sacred values, corporations acquire superprofits, generals acquire bases, and diplomats and propagandists acquire extraordinary influence, perhaps that is only a manifestation of the Biblical truth that to him who hath shall be given.

The leaders of a great nation-state need more than power; they also need the comfortable conviction that they represent the noblest possible ideas. The Protestant ethic regards with blue-eyed astonishment those cynics who smile ironically at this marriage of good conscience and material advantage. Perhaps that is why America's self-image (both popular and intellectual) is so pervaded by liberal moralism.

Seen from here in Budapest, America's democracy and its versatile liberal economy seem rather attractive. At the same time, it is remarkable how little America has done for the spread of democracy. Democracy is found today in those places where it would have existed anyway—where, after the collapse of fascism, internal political dynamics would themselves have vindicated the democratic alternative, or where the European idea of freedom was able to build upon local traditions and society's demands.

In those place, however, where the Americans found undemocratic regimes of various kinds—monarchies, fascistoid military dictatorships, and the like—they were content with military and economic cooperation, and regarded the poverty and oppression of the people as an internal affair of their clients. Indeed, in those countries where democratic popular movements or political elites mobilized autonomous forces—where the nationalism of the poor nations struggled to win independence from both superpowers—the

Americans strove for no less than the suppression of those aspirations for autonomy.

So far as we East Central Europeans are concerned, we have learned that de facto America recognizes Soviet hegemony over our area. It supports strivings for autonomy (whether successful or unsuccessful) only insofar as they can be exploited for propaganda purposes to counter centrifugal tendencies in the American camp.

Dissidents—autonomous intellectuals—are the same the world over, irrespective of their political philosophies. Whenever they chance to meet, they know one another by instinct. But I would think twice about exchanging the position of a Hungarian dissident for that of a Turkish or Southeast Asian or Latin American dissenter. It is possible that, in their shoes, I might long ago have been turned over for torture or even killed. No doubt American liberals are aware of this and no doubt they deplore it as well.

Recently we witnessed an attempt to make defense of human rights the ideological leading edge of American foreign policy, as a dramatic response to the limitation of human rights in the Soviet-type countries. Today, however, the American government is gradually removing human rights from the agenda; *Realpolitik* has triumphed over idealism. Meanwhile the ideologues declare that human rights violations are less serious if they happen in friendly countries rather than communist ones.

As I write these lines, American politicians are being moved to profound moral indignation by the violation of human rights in Poland, while Soviet politicians are being moved to profound moral indignation by the violation of human rights in El Salvador. This all-too-evident selectivity can only move the observer to profound cynicism about the moral rhetoric of the superpowers. It also suggests that we cannot expect our freedom from either of them, for neither one is particularly interested in our freedom. We can expect freedom only from ourselves, from our own patient, stubborn efforts to win it.

NUCLEAR BALANCE: A PRESENT AND FUTURE IMPOSSIBILITY

In the course of the past three decades it has become clear that the nuclear balance of terror is not a balance but an endless, unstoppable spiral. Overtly or covertly, one side always gets the upper hand, whereupon the other rushes to catch up and then presses ahead; then the first party in turn rushes to catch up and eventually gets ahead, and so on ad infinitum. Arms limitation talks are landings on the spiral staircase of weapons development, useful as platforms for propaganda; they are tactical pauses to draw breath before the next round of qualitative advances, before another sprint in the race. As a result, it becomes possible to destroy the world twice, ten times, twenty times over, and the edifice of terror rises ever higher.

The two sides don't trust each other, and each tries to trick the other. They cannot even agree on the description and evaluation of existing weapons; in converting destructive force into abstract units, they minimize their own forces and maximize those of the adversary. If one side offers a concession, the other suspects some trap behind it. If the development of one type of weapon stops, we can be sure some more up-to-date means of destruction is in the works.

On both sides, the foreign-policy strategy of the 1960s has proved unsuccessful. Its essence, it seems to me, was to talk of military balance while quietly trying to achieve primacy. This strategy has not enabled either side to gain definitive world superiority over the other. The Russians failed because the economic and technical potential of their adversary was too great. But the Americans didn't succeed either, because the Soviet system can divert a larger portion of the national income to armaments.

The other strategic goal was to acquire foreign-policy advantage, bases, and allies for use against the adversary. Over the years both sides have won many points, but both have also lost a good many. Twenty years have passed, and neither superpower has gotten the better of the other. Nor has the style of the contest become any more sophisticated: the Reagan-Andropov match is no great advance over the Kennedy-Khrushchev match. The same thing strikes us whether we look at the economies of the two great nations, or at their culture or their political intelligence: the confrontation, it seems, has not been fruitful.

The main trend of the past two decades has been the growth of the desire for independence in the intervening areas—Europe and the Third World. Local ideologies are beginning to reject the role of faithful ally. New ethnic-national identities are appearing everywhere, old and long-faded identities are reviving, allies and satellites are becoming more and more unreliable from the standpoint of both superpowers. Autonomous local forces are growing. Yesterday's flunkies have become surer of themselves; they must be dealt with as equal, sovereign partners.

The superpower strategy of the 1960s and 1970s was incoherent because it was out of step with basic historical trends and with the realities of today's world. It was anachronistic precisely because it was a superpower strategy. Try as it may, there is no way for any nation-state, however large, to seize the role of world leadership over other jealous nation-states. An imperial world order, however benevolent and peace-loving, is as futile an enterprise as were the ambitions of Napoleon and Hitler to unite Europe under their rule. The dream of a *Pax Americana* or a *Pax Sovietica* is a sure road to world conflagration, for such a peace would have to be imposed by either one side or the other, and the general staffs would determine which side it would be.

The superpowers' steps are hesitant; they follow events rather than initiate them, they save what can be saved, they never learn from each other's mistakes; their leaderships are sclerotic and devoid of imagination. The fact that the two poles of the bipolar world model are intellectually stagnant while other areas are flourishing intellectually is a sign that the bipolar model itself is obsolete. American superiority came to grief before the nationalism of a small Asian people; now Soviet superiority too is being called into question by the nationalism of a small Asian people.

The nations of Eastern Europe have chosen a road that leads toward gradual and peaceful recovery of independence. There is no other road, as the peoples of East Central Europe have learned from the lessons administered to them repeatedly, at twelve-year intervals. Their more impetuous efforts to regain their freedom have been stopped by Soviet intervention or by military dictatorship inspired and supported by the Soviets, without any effective counteraction from the West. What *Realpolitik* seems to be telling us, from both East and West, is that we can loosen our bonds only to the extent that the Soviet Union can accept some gentle relaxation without suffering injury to its prestige.

In Western Europe, the majority of the population has accepted the presence of American troops, on condition that America defend Western Europe if necessary but not plunge the region into any sort of military adventure. Over the past thirty years these two conditions have grown more problematical and perplexing. It is perfectly possible that America might refuse to risk nuclear war for the sake of Western Europe's independence. It is also possible that the United States might prefer to respond to some Soviet military aggression not with long-range strategic weapons but with medium-range theater weapons (including nuclear ones). And of course Europe would be the theater, and involved to such an extent that whole nations might vanish from the continent. In Western Europe quite a few people say they cannot imagine any political evil so great that nuclear war—even a limited one—would be a rational way to avert it.

In the Soviet-American match there are many who cheer for the American side, but I don't know anyone here in Budapest who would be willing to see our city become a battleground, even if they knew that the Americans would be here afterward. More likely there would be no one here; we would vanish along with the Russians. But we would like to stay. So if atomic war is the only thing that would get the Russians out of here, why, let them stay a while longer.

Let's try to civilize each other. Let's try to give some real meaning to the official euphemism which speaks of "the forces that are temporarily staying in our country as guests."

It is possible that trouble in the less stable areas of the world, leading to conflict between the superpowers, might set in motion the war machines that face each other in Europe. What European can imagine a Middle East or Persian Gulf conflict for which he would give his life? In recent years our patron powers have put pressure on us to help them expand their influence over parts of the world where conflicts have broken out. Meanwhile, Helsinki was an exchange of declarations with no binding force on anyone, and the Vienna talks on the mutual reduction of forces in Europe are meaningless to the point of absurdity.

Western Europe's political systems allow aspirations for neutrality to emerge openly. It hardly seems necessary to argue that if the population of Eastern Europe were to decide by referendum between neutrality and the Warsaw Pact, the majority would vote for neutrality. It seems to me that when Europeans speak freely, without the self-censorship that attends public statements, they generally express a preference for remaining neutral in any Russian-American armed conflict (an eventuality that is scarcely imaginable today without atomic weapons). This fundamental desire for neutrality is obscured by a foreign-policy rhetoric heavily influenced by our present military allies. Nevertheless, it is the subtext of European identity, and in actual fact it is more realistic than any foreign-policy strategy based merely on existing attitudes.

Even less convincing are the accusations of cowardice leveled at Europeans (whether by the Soviets or the Americans), for it is quite likely that the accusers themselves cannot conceive of any political misfortune worse than nuclear annihilation. The writers and officials who charge the Europeans with appeasement don't really know what they're talking about, I sometimes feel. I don't question their strategic expertise, but I wonder if they have seriously thought through the philosophical choices behind the strategic ones.

Many signs lead me to believe that the Western European peace movement will be followed by a new Eastern European peace movement, one not run by the Party states of the Soviet bloc. Its spokesmen will demand bilateral disarmament and will seek to extend to Eastern Europe the proposal which the Soviet President made to Western Europe—that our countries should be neither the site nor the target of nuclear weapons.

The Soviet side rejoices at the Western peace movement; the American side gloats over the Polish crisis. Each hopes that the other bloc is beginning to break up. Each is annoyed at signs of disintegration within its own bloc.

In the interests of the people of Eastern Europe, Western European neutrality should not be unilateral; we too ought to join in it. Our interests demand that Western Europe not regard its own neutrality as assured until the neutrality of Eastern Europe is guaranteed by treaty. In that way the interests of both Europes would be served, for by removing the Iron Curtain we would do away with a divisive force that is also potentially explosive.

I hope that more and more Europeans will come to

understand that the key to peace is not disarmament but the mutual withdrawal of military forces. Peace is first and foremost a political question, not a question of weapons technology. Peace is a qualitative rather than a quantitative matter.

The possibility of our continent's destruction cannot be hidden from our eyes by phrases about Atlantic loyalty or the socialist community of nations. By comparison with the alternatives of destruction or survival, the game between the Kremlin and the White House is a frivolous one. The generals may act like very serious men indeed, but their seriousness is the gravity of children absorbed in playing with their toy soldiers.

Today the world is not what it was in 1945. In the nuclear era the political doctrines of the prenuclear age are irrelevant. It may be that today new strategic shifts are ripening, for the age of the superpowers is waning. In 1955, Europe saw a wise measure taken: the signing of the Austrian State Treaty. Here was a model for resolving the problems left behind by World War II. Today Austria is no problem for either the United States or the Soviet Union. Neither fears Austria, and both derive benefit from its existence.

There are many types of neutrality: we can speak of Swiss, Swedish, Austrian, Finnish, and Yugoslav neutrality, with small but significant differences among them. It is worth noting that the Swiss, the Swedes, and the Yugoslavs are in no way less well prepared for a possible Soviet invasion than the NATO countries are. Having foregone any nuclear shield, they rely on their traditional strengths, organizing popular defense units to conduct guerrilla operations in the event of occupation—unlike the NATO countries, grown complacent in the shadow of the American nuclear umbrella.

Today it is difficult to occupy a country that has enough antitank and antihelicopter weapons, and a large popular defense force trained for protracted guerrilla warfare. Today a nuclear strategy offers more risk than security. Europe's security and defense lie with its people.

IDEOLOGICAL WAR: THE CRIPPLING METAPHYSIC OF OUR TIME

Thinking Europeans question the right of the superpower elites to decide upon the total destruction of our continent. Society's defenselessness before the state is embodied most brutally in nuclear weaponry. A European movement for emancipation has begun, and it will inevitably become a movement against Yalta. Young Europeans can no longer regard it as normal that the two superpower elites should have the privilege of turning Europe into a heap of ashes within seconds.

If liberal and communist rationalism—the two prevailing political doctrines of modern civilization—can guarantee only this extraordinarily fragile kind of security four decades after the end of World War II, we must conclude that the philosophies of the industrial world are inadequate. Our political cultures, East and West, have failed the test. The bipolar military world system of Washington and Moscow is a dangerous makeshift, to which Europe may one day fall victim.

Although both superpowers regard it as the gravest offense for someone to "drive a wedge" between them and their European allies, it seems to me that we Europeans can best safeguard the lives and security of Russians and Americans by extricating ourselves from their noisy quarrels. Staking our future on the outcome of a conflict between them— by betting on a Russian or an American victory—would hardly be worth the increased risk of nuclear war.

The undisputed hegemony of the state over society is manifested in the fact that the state possesses nuclear forces or consents to an alliance that can take the country into nuclear war. It is no exaggeration to say that atomic weapons perform a police function: the opposed blocs mutually intimidate each other's populations. The balance of terror, mutual deterrence, the conventional military balance, the military status quo of the Warsaw Pact and the NATO alliance together serve to police and intimidate society.

The leaders' propaganda declares that they are arming against each other. In reality, however, a different picture seems to present itself: it is as if the two strongest nation-states to emerge from World War II, the Soviet Union and the United States, had made an agreement to keep the rest of the world under their power and influence. Russian-American confrontation and cooperation—the Cold War— is the new Holy Alliance. Bipolar power forces societies to submit to the discipline of one bloc or the other and to varying—significantly varying—degrees of paternalism and force. Two different types of hierarchical system weigh upon society, and their ultimate police sanction is the machinery of war, which in the last analysis means atomic weapons. The Soviet bomb guarantees the police discipline of the West; the American bomb guarantees the police discipline of the East.

The post-1945 status quo has been interpreted in terms of the mentality of another era, the prenuclear age. In the nuclear era, however, the ultimate sanctions of great-power nationalism are no longer usable against the purported enemy; the war machine dare not be used to make war, since both sides shrink from global Armageddon, so the machine serves to intimidate not one's rival but one's own population. The military are a police force. Poland must have grasped this fact quite clearly on December 13, 1981. It is possible that the people of many Latin American countries view the matter in the same light.

According to an ideology still widely accepted today (though not always articulated), great nation-states have a right to try to maintain or expand their spheres of influence. The Soviet Union calls the United States an imperialist power and the United States calls the Soviet Union an imperialist power, and their propaganda makes a strong case for both sides being right. Perhaps the European states are no better, but they are less dangerous because they have less power. The anachronistic pattern of great-power spheres of influence has less and less place in European political thinking. It is beginning to be as old-fashioned as the cult of the patriarchal family or the right of a master craftsman to cuff his apprentices. It is time for Europe to speak up as an independent agent in the debate between America and the Soviet Union.

Every country's historical tradition works to transform organizational patterns imported from abroad. Thus it can

be said that the Germans have thoroughly Germanified
American organizational patterns, while the Japanese have
thoroughly Japanized them. Thanks to Yalta and Potsdam
we Hungarians were presented with organizational patterns
of the Russian type, closer in origin to the models of Asiatic
military society. Like it or not, that was what fell to our lot.
We tried to crawl out from under the authoritarian edifice
of the Central European, Austro-German empire, and we
blundered into the arms of the authoritarian Eastern empire. In the end we got Stalin in place of Hitler.

Europe's historical reality demands richer organizational
forms than those offered by the moralistic dichotomy of
American capitalism and Russian communism. Both here
and in the West, the world is divided into good boys and
bad boys: there, democracy is good and communism is bad;
here, socialism is good and capitalism is bad. We are forced
to take part in this banal and demagogic ideological war,
which goes on just as raucously as the arms race.

The East-West dichotomy makes it nearly impossible to
be clearsighted in today's world; it draws in and swallows up
good minds and mutually stupefies the world's peoples, de-
livering them over to the mercy of their political classes.
The East-West dichotomy doesn't depict the world realisti-
cally; it works ideologically, to justify the bipolar Holy
Alliance of the Cold War. In the realms of ideological war,
everything becomes uncertain; agreements no longer have
validity, and all declarations become propaganda statements. People hear what the foreign ministers say in public,
but not what they say to one another in private. The ideological war calls into being societies that are half-informed,
banal, accustomed to thinking in clichés.

Our poor dear tyrant Mátyás Rákosi* once pounded the
table at a meeting of the Hungarian politburo and asked:
"Comrades, have we sunk so low as to be taken in by our
own propaganda?" There are certainly cases of this even
today. I fear that the elderly Presidents who speak with such
consistent rudeness of each other's intentions have come to
believe what they say. They are not such sophisticated intel-
lects as to be able to think simultaneously on two different
ideological levels.

Both halves of Europe live under the influence of Yalta,
but in its tutelage Western Europe has done better. Its level
of prosperity and freedom is higher; in civil life and the
contest of attractive goods and symbols, the West is stronger.
Hungarians are Western-oriented in their travels, their personal ties and correspondence, their culture, and their
emigration. No one emigrates eastward. In our tutelage, we
have not done so well with the Eastern empire.

I am neither a communist nor an anticommunist, neither
a capitalist nor an anticapitalist; if one must absolutely be
for and against something, I consider a permanently open
democracy to be the greatest good, and the ideological war
that constantly casts the shadows of atomic war on the wall
to be the greatest evil. Ideological war speaks a language of
sensationalism; on all sides it continually stuffs minds meant
for better things full of lies and half-truths. Ideological war
is the chief occupation of second-rate intellectuals, although
it sometimes gains power over better minds as well.

Peacemaking is not a phrase to me; to my mind, it implies

---

* The confirmed Stalinist who ruled Hungary from 1947 to 1956, when he
fled to the Soviet Union in the wake of the Hungarian revolution. [Pub-
lisher's note.]

reflection, introspection, and cultural criticism of the most intensive kind. We must always bear clearly in mind that human aggressiveness is incredibly ingenious. It incessantly generates new collective attitudes, all of which sound frightfully moral, yet somehow they all come down to the fact that regrettably, even tragically, realistic wisdom dictates that we have to kill these or those people. The proliferation of homicidal and suicidal sensibilities is the devil's work that aggressiveness performs in our cultures.

The time has come to create some sort of spiritual order between East and West. The time has come to examine, with the greatest possible seriousness and good humor, just why the hundreds of millions of vassals of the Kremlin and the White House are arming against each other. I find the mythology of the ideological war as irrational as the medieval dualism of heaven and hell. Our rational age is feeding on fairy tales. Russians and Americans alike delude themselves with the most terrible imaginings of all. They must decide whether they want to be great nation-states or rule the world. If they want to be no more than what they are—great nation-states—then we can live in peace and get on to the real issue: the tensions between North and South. If they want to be more than they are, if they think this tiny globe was made for them, if they puff themselves up like Aesop's frog, then millions of us are going to be blown away when the inevitable explosion comes.

Our ideological differences are ridiculous compared to the difference between hunger and abundance. We have a moral obligation to expose the spendthrift squabbles of the well-fed for the elemental madness they are, when hundreds of millions are dying before their time from malnourishment.

If there is a Soviet ideology and an American ideology, why shouldn't there be a European ideology, too? No one has a better chance of making an impact on the two great powers. It is up to Europe to draw them into an intelligent dialogue, to bring the Russian and American elites together face to face, to help influential Russians and Americans learn to talk to each other without propaganda preconceptions, without fancy demagoguery, and without the primitive need to triumph over the other fellow. If they can't yet talk this way publicly, let them do it in small private groups. Let European and American academics meet in Europe, with the TV cameras absent, without any worldwide publicity. Let them sit down together in the Caffé Florian in Venice, where a great European, Friedrich Nietzsche, loved to sit, and talk quietly and sincerely with each other.

If we don't think about the conditions for peace, then our countries will be of interest to the world and its news media only as potential bases and targets for nuclear weapons. I am pleased that our Western European friends are also beginning to be afraid. I am glad they are beginning to feel that their lives too are at stake. Now they can experience what we on this side of the Iron Curtain have experienced. If they are not careful—if they remain trapped in a foolish professionalism that separates politics from other aspects of intellectual life—they may find that history will walk into their studies one day and grab them by the throat. History may castigate them and burn them to dust.

If this prospect gives them pause, let them make the most

of the opportunities afforded them by their liberties, which far exceed our own. If we don't draw the two halves of Europe closer together, we will be fighting tank battles with each other instead. Our tanks are many and can overrun a city most disagreeably. Think of the Iron Curtain, look at the Berlin Wall: you will feel the pathos of our continent in all its poignancy.

WHAT DO THE RUSSIANS WANT: TO WIN OR TO SETTLE?

Both great powers are tempted, from time to time, by the option of global victory—the strategy of a worldwide offensive. The Russians, of course, are no strangers to this temptation. What has the dream of world revolution been ever since October 1917, if not a vision of world domination by the Third Rome, the Moscow of the true communist faith? Marxist-Leninist revolutionism of the Bolshevik variety is the export rhetoric of Russian imperialism.

Today this is clearer than ever, as more details come to light about the Red Army Faction, the Red Brigades, the Latin American guerrillas, the PLO, and other anti-imperialist, ultraradical groups that espouse armed insurrection and liberation through terrorism (officially disavowed in Eastern Europe); or the Libyan secret police, organized on the Soviet and East German model; or the Hungarian, Czech, East German, and especially Soviet training camps for guerrillas and terrorists; or above all, the export of arms from Eastern Europe.

Ugly though it may sound when the Americans label all this as international terrorism—and true though it may be that the Palestine issue and the Salvadoran civil war cannot be reduced to the machinations of Soviet agents—it is also clear that in a bipolar world the two sides in a local conflict can be reduced by the logic of the situation to being agents of the two great powers, agents simultaneously sincere and bought.

All this revolutionary phraseology, which—as we can see here in Eastern Europe—no longer has any real basis in the countries where socialism is said to have been achieved, has little to do with any utopia; but it has everything to do with the conspiratorial foreign expansion of the Soviet system. All the revolutionary rhetoric is merely instrumental in character; it is a tool of Soviet global expansion, geared to serving the Soviet option of victory.

Soviet expansion seems to come in waves. There are times when it revives, and other times when it is dormant. During the pauses, one may think that the Russians are only waiting for the next advance, but it is also thinkable that at such times they are uncertain whether they are on the right track. It seems realistic to suppose that the civilian and military policy makers who influence and finally make the decisions must sometimes wonder (though not in public) what their country's relationship to the rest of the world is and ought to be.

I hardly think that Russian policy makers are crackpots, or men possessed, or ideological fanatics. They are mature, dry, stolid, cautious, mistrustful men; they don't want to come out losers in the game. They don't want to be forced into a corner or see their country humiliated. Their historical experience has been one of being regarded with suspicion, of being encircled and attacked. It is almost as if they believe that expansion is necessary for defense. Lest the enemy attack the frontiers, buffer states must be created on every frontier. They occupied half of Poland so as to have a buffer there to absorb any blow—and sure enough, the blow followed.

Anyone in politics has to understand the other side's neuroses; it is not enough to scold the other fellow because he won't behave, because he wants something different. Fear of occupation is a Russian historical reflex, hence they would rather be the ones to do the occupying. For a long time they were under the occupation of Tartar khans; Ivan the Great, Ivan the Terrible, and Peter the Great succeeded in defending their independence against Tartars, Turks, Poles, and Swedes only by attacking and expanding, while their people multiplied and settled the great empty spaces of the Russian plain, Siberia, and Central Asia. The Russian state stretched out toward Central Europe and reached down into Central Asia, lest the enemy occupy Moscow. This people that had to fight for its independence learned too much from its occupiers, the Tartar khans, and ever since winning independence has never felt secure in its possession. Constantly jealous of its independence and suspicious of others, it has not shrunk from perfidy.

After that came Westernization and a new orientation toward Europe. And what did they get from the West? They got Napoleon and Hitler and, in time of peace, a full measure of disdain, condescension, and fear; they were regarded as barbaric, rude, stupid, unpolished.

They spoke French, but French rationalism struck shallow roots in their souls. Reading the two greatest European writers of the nineteenth century, Tolstoy and Dostoyevsky, we can see how it is possible to regard Western Europe as the Eldorado of the petty bourgeois—a soulless civilization of insensitive, parsimonious rationalists, fussy pedants, individualists indifferent toward their fellow man and the community, where prosperity and technique may be found, but not happiness or salvation, where normality exists but not exaltation.

One need only read what they write about the French, and what the French write about them, to feel the profound lack of comprehension between these two nations, allied for so long in foreign policy and linked by longstanding cultural ties. Here two national identities attracted to each other—and for that very reason unintelligible to each other —asserted themselves forcefully. It is fitting to cite the French-Russian tie because it is the most obvious and symbolic East-West relationship in Europe.

Any historic compromise between Russians and Europeans must be preceded by understanding between two cultures, two kinds of reason. It is necessary to understand how Dostoyevsky's relationship to the West differs from Stalin's, and how it is akin to it. Today there is no Tolstoy and no Dostoyevsky. There is only Solzhenitsyn, a giant in his writings on the gulag, to be sure, but also a writer who has never outgrown the conceptual matrix of Russian Orthodox nationalist ideology; in his work the passion for judgment outruns the passion to understand. He has not tried to understand the West, or America as a part of it, and this may inspire doubts about how well he has been able to understand his own country. Who will come after Solzhenitsyn? Who will be the independent Russian thinker who will make a historic proposal to both the West and the Russian power elite, telling them how Russians and Europeans can live with each other?

After the initial difficulties of the post-Stalin period, the Russians took heart and devised a two-pronged strategy. On the interstate level, they called for détente: mutual respect for frontiers and for the sovereignty of the power elites over the populations within them. On the other hand, they carried out a substantial arms buildup and strove to keep up the ideological war. In the ideological sphere, they have often said, there is no peaceful coexistence. They want to maintain the world revolutionary movement as well, by supporting so-called national liberation movements, primarily through the export of weapons, ideology, and advisers—the technology of winning and retaining power.

This strategy was all the more attractive at the time because the colonial empires of the European middle powers were disintegrating, and the movements and states of the uncommitted world were making their clamorous entry onto the world stage. It is perfectly understandable that this soft, rich morsel attracted Russian policy-makers. What if it were possible to encircle Atlantic civilization with a ring of anti-imperialist countries? What if it were possible to tighten the ring around Western Europe and North America? Suppose that imperialism could be cut off from its raw materials and energy supplies? Could the strategic confrontation be won on the world market instead? Could politics triumph over economics? Could world communism beat world capitalism by means of a great anti-imperialist coalition of the Soviet bloc and the Third World?

Support for Idi Amin or Colonel Qaddafi, indirect support for terrorists—these were only the incidental means adopted, now shrewdly, now foolishly, in carrying out this two-pronged strategic option: in Europe, détente and the slow neutralization of Western Europe; in the soft underside of the world, armed expansion by means of surrogates. It cannot be said that the Americans remained idle in the meantime. They lost in Vietnam, they won in Egypt—the shifting fortunes of war. But to return to the Russians: they became overconfident, they spread their nets too far. They gambled too much and spent too much on the means of expansion, which cost too much and brought in too little. In pursuing the dual option, the Russians miscalculated. They never decided what they wanted: to win or to settle.

Afghanistan, it appears, was the last stop for this sometimes successful train of expansion efforts. With their intervention there, the Russians blundered into a hornets' nest. They brought more trouble on themselves than any profit they have reaped. The invasion of Afghanistan—the strategic highway to the oil resources of the Persian Gulf—reminded the West that the Russians are impelled by longer-range strategic and military considerations.

Not everything that the analysts of the Reagan administration say is unfounded. The new medium-range missiles, the expanded navy, the transfer of national income to military purposes at the cost of squeezing domestic consumption

—all this suggests that the Soviet leaders still consider the option of victory to be at least as valid as the option of a settlement with America. The disquieting convergence of the civil and military apparatus, the silencing of the democratic opposition, the unbending severity toward protests over emigration restrictions, the inability to give any real autonomy to the peasants (even though more production is needed from their plots) or to the industrial enterprises (even though an efficient, high-quality industry is needed just as much)—this too suggests that the Russian elite is more concerned with external power than with domestic prosperity. It is also true that when America displays strength the Russians become more moderate, and when America shows weakness the Russians begin to flex their muscles again. All of these truths are reason enough why America should show strength. It is not, however, an argument for America in its turn to adopt a strategy of global victory.

America should offer a settlement to those present or future Russian leaders who are themselves inclined to prefer a settlement to a strategy of victory, with the excessive risk and trouble and the dubious benefits that such a strategy entails. It would be up to that hypothetical group in the leadership to make a case before the Soviet elite for a settlement, in opposition to arguments for the possibility of victory. The West, if it is sensible, will help them. How? By formulating the terms and the stakes of a settlement clearly and honestly; by making a straightforward business proposition. If the West responds to the two-pronged Soviet strategy with a two-pronged strategy of its own, then it will be making the same mistake as the Russians.

If the Soviet bloc tried to live in isolation, eliminating Western influence in all areas, then trade too would cease and how would we pay our debts? The socialist camp would simply find itself in the ridiculous position of owing the West $90 billion which it couldn't begin to repay. ("Socialist camp"—what an expression! After the prison camps of Kolyma and Magadan, what can they expect people to think of?)

It turns out that the world market is stronger than the isolationist tendencies of the empire. We have so many tanks that we can even use them on our own people and still have enough to meet the needs of starving countries for armor, even if we can't send them food. Sooner or later it becomes painfully apparent that we have here all sorts of lethal gadgets, easily fired off, and we don't know what to do with them; but at the same time the things that the residents of the camp need (a few lucky areas aside) are in chronic short supply.

We are behind in our debts and may never pay them off. We are taking out loans in order to pay the interest on old loans. Like indignant poor relations, we complain when our rich relative—whom otherwise we try to infuriate in every way possible—refuses to let us sponge off him any longer. It is revolting to see the TV commentator's face as he pretends to be scandalized because our enemies will not support us—more proof of how wicked they are! Let's be clear about whom we're dealing with here—our enemy, or our rich uncle? If the other side has more of all the things we need, why should we puff ourselves up, claiming to be on a par with him and equally strong?

If we could give up this stupid and hypocritical delusion,

we could come to grips with the fact that we are the poorer ones. And because we are, we have no business being in an arms race which only leaves us poorer still. What do the Russian marshals want from us anyway? Do they want the Hungarians to overrun Germany, Italy, and France, passing through neutral Austria along the way? Is there any sign that those countries want to attack us? If not, why the devil do we have to maintain this costly, overblown, empty bluff of a Warsaw Pact?

What do we want from the Russians? To overcome the sclerosis of their institutions and get on, belatedly, with their real business: after long decades of bluffly avoiding the issue, to set about social and economic reform. For centuries they have postponed the task of nonviolent renewal, like a doctor who refuses to loosen a tight bandage to permit the blood to circulate again.

In the nineteenth century they were the last to emancipate the serfs; it was Nicholas I's chief distinction that he managed to put it off for another generation. The present leadership's chief distinction is that it has succeeded in putting off the emancipation of the citizenry. Today's leadership is capable of outfitting agriculture with fantastic technical investments, but unable to legislate the emancipation of the kolkhoz peasantry.

Less idolatry of technology would still be more than enough if coupled with more respect for individuals. There will be plenty of grain and computer chips, too, when the propaganda photos distributed abroad no longer show Russians dressed with such depressing frequency in uniforms: workers, scouts, athletes, folk dancers—all in uniform, not to mention the army and police. We see the masses, superbly trained, all performing the very same action. At their sports festivals thousands of children, each a piece in the mosaic, mass together to form messages of homage to the elderly gentlemen in identical hats who sit on the dignitaries' platform.

Has it never occurred to them how ludicrously revealing their most official publications are to people who think differently? Perhaps they are no longer able—or not yet able —to see themselves with civilian eyes. Perhaps militarized Soviet man looks like this to himself. Even in the buff he remains the uniformed soldier of Party and state. But when I see the young Russian, Ukrainian, and Tadzhik recruits here in Hungary, lounging at their posts or wandering around the railroad stations, returning perhaps from leave, I feel that these are only sad and resigned young men who could get along very well without the marshals and their grandeur.

The Soviet leaders must decide how much they should encourage tendencies toward integration of the empire, and how much the tendencies toward its differentiation. They must decide, in other words, whether to define it as primarily a European or an Asiatic power. What will receive priority over the long run—intensive development of the economy, or military adventures? I hardly think that those about to relieve the septuagenarian guard at the highest levels of state will be able to evade this dilemma. The decision is made more difficult by the fact that the Soviet bloc, if it chooses peace, must rest content with being a second-rate economic power. In the competition for the works of peace, we have not kept pace. The productive capacity of the Soviet civilian economy is no greater than Japan's and considerably less than Western Europe's.

In destructive capacity, the Soviet Union is on a par with even the United States. Ambitious old politicians like to compete, too, and if they can choose the arena of competition they will choose the one where they have the greatest chance of success, not the one where they are weaker. Since destruction is cheaper than construction—since in the nuclear era each unit of investment in military production yields an exponential increase in destructive capacity—it is possible for the Soviet Union to be just as dangerous as the United States, even though it cannot be as rich. At least it cannot be as rich so long as, feeling inferior, it seeks the cheaper kind of equality, military equality, rather than the more expensive kind, attained through development of the civilian economy.

The 1980s will decide which is more important for the Soviet elite: civilian reality or military appearance. If the Soviet leaders could say: "We are what we are, we stand where we stand, what we want is to have a better life; we would rather be loved than feared; we are strong enough so no one would want to attack us"—if the Soviet leadership talked like this, then we could believe that Russia is governed not just by old men, but by grown men as well.

The present Russian leadership is unable to pull itself together, unable to take advantage of the political wisdom of the Russian intelligentsia. No one can believe the contrary so long as there are political prisoners in the Soviet Union, and new ones being locked up all the time on charges of anti-Soviet propaganda. The military option is an expression of the leadership's insecurity over the fact that the Soviet people are able to hold their own in the world, as individuals, without direction or leadership from above— and not just in uniform, in organized ranks, according to the manual of arms. The military option implies censorship; it makes clearsightedness impossible and secrecy mandatory. The military option rejects constitutional relationships, rejects bargaining and negotiation between higher and lower state organs and between the state and its citizens. The military option excludes both internal and external publics from deliberations on the most fundamental questions at issue in society. The military option rejects precisely the two values basic to democracy and civil society: autonomy and solidarity. The military option perpetuates itself by stultifying the minds of the Soviet people, forbidding them to discuss freely, as masters of their own destiny and country, where they are headed—toward hyperarmament or peace.

Critical thinking about peace and an independent peace movement are needed in the Soviet Union, if they are needed anywhere in the world. Those who choose peace choose reform and democracy. Those who choose to overarm choose the inefficiency, the squalor, and the inflexibility of post-Stalinist centralization (still all too Stalinist in its essentials). A nation is choosing between two fundamentally different profiles. It is a decisive question for Europe whether the Russian elite has committed itself permanently and irrevocably to the military option. Can we hope that it has enough confidence in itself and in Soviet society to address its internal and external tasks creatively? Does our fate depend on whether the Russian leadership chooses peace with its own people and with other countries?

HISTORIC COMPROMISE IN EUROPE: LIFTING THE IRON CURTAIN

The time has come to put compromise on the agenda—a historic compromise between the Soviet Union and the other European states, between the Russian people and the other peoples of Europe, between communists and non-communists. The Russians have a right to security and friendship, but no right to any sort of imperialism. The Russians are a great people, but if they want to rule over Europe they will be destroyed in the attempt (while destroying many other peoples, it is true).

It's because of the Cold War that the Russians prevent us Eastern Europeans from exercising our right of self-determination. In peacetime the Americans don't stand in the way of Western Europeans' self-determination; they limit it only insofar as they may at any time take Western Europe into nuclear war. To simplify greatly, Soviet restraints are actual, American restraints only potential.

It is not our aim to exchange our actual limited self-determination for the potential kind. We cannot belong to any military alliance at all if we keep our real security interests firmly in view. In this unsettled world, we cannot allow ourselves to be drawn into war because client interests have been damaged somewhere in the Middle East or Far East. If the Russians or their voluntary clients get into a war of prestige somewhere or other, that shouldn't affect us. If there is a fire in the neighborhood, we should act as a fire-break, not add more fuel. Let us, as independent Eastern Europeans, start a dialogue with independent Western Europeans. If people on both sides of the Iron Curtain merely act as faithful allies, we will not be able to prevent a collision of the two great powers. We help them most by preparing the way for agreement through frank, open discussion.

If America wants to win, we want no part of that. We are not interested in any victory that might lead to civil war in the lands east of the Iron Curtain. All we should want, if we pursue our own interests strictly, is a genuine compromise. I say it once again: Eastern European communists must accept the democratic practice of Western European communism, and must do so in a Europe where there are neither Russian nor American troops, neither Russian nor American nuclear missiles.

The least we could sincerely wish for ourselves is the degree of freedom that Finland enjoys. And of course neutrality: our national interests don't demand that we abandon our military alliance with Moscow only to join with Washington in a pact directed against the Soviet Union.

Indeed, we want to avoid the necessity of ever having to fire on Russian soldiers again. Hungarians fired on Russians in World War II and they were wrong to do so. They were just as wrong to move into the Ukraine as the Russians were wrong to occupy half our country in 1849 in order to crush the Hungarian struggle for independence. Hungarians fired on Russians in 1956; once again we found ourselves at war with them. Their tanks put an end to our twelve days of self-determination. If they had not done so, we would be living in friendship now with the Soviet Union, like Finland or Austria. If we want to ensure once and for all that twenty-year-old Russians and twenty-year-old Hungarians with no mutual grudge will never fire on one another again, we should conclude a treaty of nonaggression and nonintervention with the Soviet Union.

Trade on a footing of equality, good-neighborly friendship, real substantive ties, and at home, self-determination. Communist ministers in the government? Fine. There are communist ministers in the Finnish government and the French government. Let there be communist ministers, in proportion to the number of votes the Communist Party wins at the elections. If its policies are as popular as those of János Kádár, there may be many communist ministers in the government.

Let Eastern European communists accept the Eurocommunist principle of pursuing socialism only within the context of democracy, and only to the extent that society voluntarily agrees to it, through a pluralistic political system. It would be easy to let a multiplicity of forms of property and rights to use it evolve, in a free yet orderly way, with the state—a democratic state—assuming a significant, indeed indispensable, role. If communists could accept democracy rather than "democratic centralism," then socialism would no longer be a crude simplification in which the state swallows up all private and civic autonomy.

As soon as it achieved nationwide scope, the Polish opposition accepted the Warsaw Pact and the Iron Curtain. We don't like the Iron Curtain, its leaders said, but for now we won't talk about it; we will remain allies of the Russians, just give us a little limited autonomy here at home. They gave it to them, but it turned out that autonomy doesn't easily tolerate limitation. Then Marshal Kulikov came, several times, then the Polish general with the tinted glasses, the savior, the centrist, the reformer, the Kádárist, who represented the spirit of Polish statehood, and with whom it would be possible to reach agreement. But what sort of agreement? A little limited autonomy? What they already had, was that too much? So now a little less? Just a tiny bit?

Better not to bestow any at all formally: we will not barter our salvation for a bowl of lentils. What we want is unlimited self-determination, unlimited democracy, unlimited freedom to speak out. Yes, we want at least as much freedom as the small nations of northwestern Europe have. Yes, we want the Russian troops to go home. If the postwar political situation demands that they be here, and now and then impose or ordain a military dictatorship, then we reject the postwar political situation. Let them go home, and we will go back (or rather forward) to the status quo that would have evolved here of its own accord, without such external disturbances as the communist seizures of power and the counterrevolutions of November 4, August 21, and December 13.

We want that internal process with which East Central Europe is already pregnant; we want bourgeois civil liberties and an embourgeoisement that is not hedged about with prohibitory decrees. We don't want the authorities to have discretionary rights over us. We want constitutional guarantees; we want it clear that semifreedom is not freedom, half-truth not truth, liberalization not liberalism, democratization not democracy. We want no less than what the most advanced democracies now have.

We will not get it by revolution. We will not get it through gradual reforms. We will not get it by a third world war. How will we get it? I see no other way except for Europe to propose to the two superpowers that they mutually withdraw from the Iron Curtain.

Someone is sure to say, "Yes, but what an upsetting of the European balance! The Russians will withdraw only to their neighboring territories, three hundred kilometers away, and could be here again with their tanks in two days. For that, are the Americans supposed to withdraw across the ocean? What will happen when the Americans are gone? The Russians, after pretending to go home, could come running back before the Americans had even reached their own shores, and could keep on going all the way to the Atlantic! Such a mutual withdrawal would mean only that the Russians would swallow up Western as well as Eastern Europe!"

Do those who think this way really believe that the Russians would feign going home only to come hurrying back again? Do the Russians really fear the symbolic presence of the tripwire force of 350,000 American troops now stationed in Western Europe? What a childish conception of the Russians! There is such a thing as childlike trust, but there is also such a thing as childlike mistrust. This line of reasoning seems paranoiacally simplistic to me. First of all, the Russians and the Americans, if they reached agreement, would have had some clear consensual basis on which to do so. That could only be the basis already accepted in international practice, at least on the rhetorical level: the principles of national sovereignty, territorial inviolability, and repudiation of aggression. On that basis, let everyone go home. The Russians cannot withdraw their troops beyond the sea because they live in Eurasia. But they can withdraw most of them beyond the Urals and reduce their numbers significantly. And most important, if there is an open and real agreement, they will have no reason to come hurrying back in an instant.

Withdrawing from Eastern Europe would be a fundamental and far-reaching political decision for the Soviet leadership. It would signal their readiness to abandon worldwide expansion and take the road of domestic reform. It would indicate that they wished to live here among the other nations of Europe according to equitable and publicly expressed principles of law. It would mean that they had reconsidered their place among the other peoples of the Eurasian land mass and now wished to assure themselves their rightful place in a spirit of equal partnership rather than domination. The least common denominator of such an agreement would be a principle of international relations whereby it would be an anomaly for one state to keep troops on the territory of another. There is no reason inherent in internal European affairs why this anomaly should be maintained in Europe any longer.

Every agreement presupposes a minimum of trust among the participants. If the West cannot trust the Soviet Union at all, then it will not be able to reach any agreement with it. It will then be obliged to proceed on the assumption that

55

the Soviet Union will break any agreement, will follow only
the logic of force, will seek only power, and will retreat only
in the face of superior power. Western strategy will be based
on the view that the Soviet Union can only be driven to the
wall and forced into collapse. Indeed, neoconservative
ideologues are saying this now.

Actually, the West also has two possible strategic options.
Between them lie a great many half-baked, ill-defined
variants, but they all come down to either the one option or
the other: the strategy of settlement or the strategy of victory. One follows a historical and political rationale, the
other a military one.

The ideological war, which attributes to the other side
the most diabolic intentions possible, can provide a theoretical justification for the military rationale and the strategy
of victory—a strategy of forcing the opponent into a corner,
threatening him with weapons until he yields, or else. Historical and political analysis of the European situation is
more complicated; military strategists are unlikely to make
it their own. Historical and political analysis is an intellectual approach that strives to see our present as if it were
already history—as the surface of the historical past.

Naturally, a more sophisticated analysis of how Russians
and Europeans might coexist won't be based upon a crude
game plan involving two gun-toting cowboys waiting for
each other in the dark. If the Russians were really not to be
trusted, the blow would already have fallen long ago. The
Russians would have swallowed up West Berlin; indeed,
the Atlantic would wash at their feet. For there was a time
when their conventional forces were superior and their
European theater missiles gave them the option of striking

first. Yet there is no real indication that the Russians ever sought such a confrontation with the Americans. They didn't seek it even when they had superiority. Nor is it true that the 350,000 American soldiers defend Western Europe from the Russians. They would only be hostages caught in a trap if the Russians really wanted to occupy Western Europe.

Ideally, the most political intelligence would be found where the greatest military and economic power is—in the United States and its political elite. It is a vital interest of ours that the Americans not be obsessed with lecture-platform self-congratulation at being the strongest, richest, freest, noblest, most unselfish nation, overreacting neurotically to every setback and every challenge, seeing intrigue, ingratitude, and communist machinations wherever other people, having interests that don't coincide with America's, insist on pursuing them anyway. Americans should understand if others act like nationalists, too; Americans shouldn't naively identify their own national interests with the happiness of all.

Let's not only tolerate but even applaud, if poor nations want to free themselves from dictatorship, if Latin Americans need democracy as much as North Americans do. We ought to learn that the peoples of the world instinctively want to be neutral in the conflicts of others—conflicts that can only cost them their lives. Why should the Americans, who can display a striking neutrality as individuals if they see someone robbed on the street or in the subway, expect that friendly nations will show solidarity unto death with them in far more threatening circumstances? I would be curious to see the courage of the neoconservatives in concrete individual situations. The American press is not serious when it lectures Europeans, with lofty moralism, about "cowardice" and "appeasement." Noted thinkers are not serious when they go on about "animal instinct," having discovered that people fear for their lives. A healthy fear of death in fact suggests more political wisdom than does the present American government's far from exclusively rational military and foreign-policy strategy.

We don't call on the Americans to be cowardly and impotent, but we do ask them to couple their strength with wisdom—more historical and political wisdom than they are showing today. They shouldn't just deter the Russians but also offer them clear and attractive alternatives. The Carter administration was soft and shortsighted toward the Russians in Eastern Europe; the Reagan administration is tough and shortsighted. Peace demands a wise policy, one that is tough and clearsighted both.

Ideally, the Americans should make a broad offer to the Russians: "You will get complete security if you give self-determination to the Eastern European countries. Between us we will permit a strong and peaceful Europe to arise, on good terms with us and with you. We are getting nowhere haggling over how many missiles you can have and how many we can have, how many of your soldiers there should be in the Warsaw Pact countries and how many of ours in the NATO countries. We will never agree on these matters if we sit and talk till we drop. We are only kidding world opinion along with these Geneva and Vienna talks. We declare reassuringly that we are going to negotiate at the highest level, or at lower levels; it's all the same, if negotiations start out from unproductive premises or follow a course that both of us know will lead nowhere. The reason we get nowhere is because you want to score and we want to score, you want to cheat us and we want to cheat you, you are jealous of your superiority and we are jealous of ours. These arms control talks are a fig leaf to conceal the fact that we both go on arming, by mutual consent. How would it be if we changed our approach and addressed essential matters? To hell with Europe—it means only trouble for you and for us. In the last analysis these are old nations, as old as we are; they will get along without our tutelage. We shouldn't be pursuing quantitative solutions but rather a European historical, political, and ideological solution. We don't mean to offend you, but really, this socialism of yours, you know, it's not so incomparably advanced. Without our grain you and your cattle wouldn't live nearly so well. You too have things to do in your own backyard. Maybe it's time to remove from your agenda the slogan which that clever fellow Khrushchev put there almost a quarter-century ago, the one about overtaking, passing, and burying us. Couldn't there still be peaceful coexistence, a few common denominators, some modest consensus between us in ideology or in the way we set our goals and priorities? That in itself would already be more than détente; it would be peace."

When I read the arguments of Reagan administration officials and sympathetic journalists now, I don't see such an offer about to emanate from the Oval Office or anyplace else in America. After Vietnam, it is understandable that the Americans would like to score a foreign policy success somewhere. The question is, in what way are they most likely to do so? It is not enough to play the tough guy, not enough to project the movie ideals of American mythology onto the complex fabric of international relations. It is not enough to talk ad infinitum of new arms deliveries, new weapons systems, strategic balance. More intelligence is needed in approaching the Russians; we cannot be content with the empty assertion that the Russians understand only force. In fact, what the Russians understand is a mutually advantageous business proposition, forcefully advanced—a proposition outlining a historic compromise between the Soviet Union and the United States.

The Soviets cannot be excluded as constructive partners from either the Middle East or Southeast Asia. If they are shut out, they will only appear on the scene again—either directly as in Afghanistan, or indirectly through the governments and movements aligned with them—to demand a part in any settlement or disturb existing arrangements. If America continually strives to push the Russians out everywhere, it will only meet with disappointment, because if the Russians don't come back in through the door they will come back in through the window; if they are not present officially and constructively, they will be there unofficially and destructively, clinging to the prestige owed a serious global partner and constantly resentful at being so rudely left out of the game.

So let them play! Let them send advisers everywhere if they have so many to spare, but let them be doctors, not soldiers, and dispatched by mutual agreement. Are there no more such advisers, no more packets of food and medicine? That would be a shame. America would indeed take a great initiative toward solving the problems of the world if it combined its efforts with those of the Russians, in the same way that the two cooperate now in research on cancer or controlled fusion energy.

THE EUROPEAN SOLUTION

Everyone shares responsibility for the untoward way our destinies have developed; no one is without blame. The moralistic indignation of the Western elites at the great-power cynicism of Russian expansion has never been free of hypocrisy. I will believe they are talking seriously when they make a business proposition to the Russians: "If you withdraw from East Central Europe, you'll get thus and so in return."

The West is not in a position to intimidate or punish the Soviet Union—it is not strong enough. In the nuclear era it can never be strong enough for that. The West can change the present status quo only if it is willing to make an attractive business proposition—if it can induce the Russians to withdraw troops while strengthening the Russians' sense of security through commensurate withdrawals of American forces from Western Europe. How Russian or American national pride would bear the withdrawal of forces I don't know. I can speak, however, for a country whose national pride has borne the weight of a good many lengthy occupations. We don't at all miss the opportunity to keep occupation troops in other countries.

I am not at all sure that the rhetoric of great-power pride is the language of wisdom. Seen from Budapest, all sentiments of national grandeur seem irredeemably comic. The comical thing is that the citizen of a big power is in no way a big man; he is a little man, every bit as much as the resident of a small country. Linking the greatness of one's person with the greatness of one's country is an odd brand of idiocy.

The great nation-states of Europe always subordinated the diverse interests of Europe to their own selfish national interests, and as a result their national importance only dwindled: they became victims. By weakening Central Europe they managed to weaken the whole of Europe as well. French domination of the European continent was no less arrogant than German domination. The end result: all Europe fell under the tutelage of the two peripheral powers.

What can Western Europeans do about it? They can integrate. The more united Western Europe is, the more self-confidence we will have here in East Central Europe. If they want to help us, let them strengthen their sense of European identity and revive the notion that Europe is the agent of its own destiny, with a strategy and political profile of its own. The new European identity will shun such historical anachronisms as the idea that one nation can rule over another. It is clear that the French, the English, and the Germans can no longer do so. Now it remains to convince the Russians that they can't either.

There is no visceral hatred among the nations of Europe. From the Urals to the Atlantic the nations look amiably on one another; they don't understand why they have to threaten one another with mutual annihilation. The opposition of the two halves of Europe is not a product of national feelings but of craven accommodation to the edifice of Yalta. Within the Yalta framework it is possible to speak only of détente, not of peace. There will be no peace between Moscow and Washington so long as there is an Iron Curtain; indeed, there cannot even be lasting détente, since both partners are afraid they may lose something which is not really theirs anyway. America lost its head because it was afraid it would lose South Vietnam. Russia lost its head because it was afraid it would lose Afghanistan. It must be an unhappy lot to be a great power, constantly going in fear of losing something.

Russians and Americans can be prevented from coming into conflict over Europe only if the European countries pursue a foreign policy of their own—that is, if the various nations of Western and East Central Europe, large and small, subordinate their relations as little as possible to the politics of great-power blocs. On the contrary, they must seek ties independently of the Soviet-American rivalry and free themselves from the rigid pattern of the East-West relationship.

We can create, within the basic structure of Yalta, relatively pluralistic political forms that approximate those of the European democracies. Our goal is to free today's Europe gradually from the post-World War II European order, from the Procrustean bed of the Cold War. Our goal is to see our political structures determined more by our real social conditions, rather than by a military status quo devised with an eye to the possibility of a third world war.

A gradual negotiated end to the Yalta system is the precondition for world peace. The independent Central European intelligentsia holds as one of its cardinal beliefs (which it offers for consideration by both East and West) that so long as the Yalta model persists, the danger of a third world war will also persist. Eastern Europe's social crises recur again and again, throwing the dictatorial elements of the Yalta system into sharper relief each time. Each suppressed bid for freedom polarizes the world political situation again. A more flexible strategy, by contrast—a strategy of gradual evolution—would lead not to a bipolar world but to a polycentric one. Polycentrism is a good thing for Europe, bipolarity is not. An adroit strategy leading to polycentrism is the only one that points the way toward a European solution.

The European solution is sensible, flexible, realistic and utopian all at once; it aims to calm nervous violence. The European solution doesn't require the language of compulsion, the ethos of struggle, the rude mentality always ready to threaten and strike out. We have outgrown the period of our history when this tone of voice was still prevalent. We don't want to brandish clubs at one another. We don't want to act like angry gorillas. We don't want to strut and boast, peeking all the while to see who is mocking us behind our backs.

The European solution is more congenial to the small nations of Europe than the outlook of large nations intent on hegemony. The small nations must teach the large ones their own more patient philosophy, lest the boastful giants start swinging at each other. European identities are emerging at a critical pace in both East and West. The mass movement against new missile deployment in Western Europe is more than just a protest against a concrete military measure; many kinds of social and cultural demands enter into its single overriding theme. It is a cry for autonomy, for the right of self-determination. We cannot allow the Soviet and American political elites to make the decisions that affect our lives. In both East and West, the European political vanguard has declared that our societies have the right to decide their own destinies.

EASTERN EUROPE IN THE STRAITJACKET OF YALTA

Yalta was a military solution to a complex of social issues. It was not based at the time—and is not based today—on any historical insight into the region it affects. The percentages, the effort to apportion Eastern and Western great-power influence for decades to come, were astonishingly naive and irrelevant, in light of the real complexity of the issues. The fundamental historical issues of Central Europe have remained unresolved ever since.

Since World War II, various types of accommodation to the status quo created by Yalta have emerged, and various attempts to shake free of it have run their course. At first Moscow saw a wholesale transfer of its own social and political system as the prerequisite for creating in the new client states a power elite whose basic interests would coincide with its own. Meanwhile, however, the model became differentiated, and the way in which it was interpreted also changed. Each local governing bureaucracy subjected the identical institutional forms to its own interpretation. With this, Yalta became a living reality, a distinct civilization in several variant versions.

Our societies were not particularly eager to belong to the Soviet world. Nowhere in East Central Europe did the majority of the population vote after World War II to belong to the Soviet rather than the Western sphere of influence. Where elections gave the people a means of expressing their wishes, the majority voted for Western-style democracy.

The Communist Parties of East Central Europe carried out a gradual coup d'état against the noncommunist and even national communist politicians with whom, until around 1948, they shared a power delegated from Moscow. Then they received from Stalin a prediction and an order. The prediction was that soon—within four or five years—World War III would break out; the order was to unify the region in every respect, under Moscow's direction, so that it would respond as directly and unconditionally as possible to military command.

It was within the context of this martial doctrine that our institutions emerged, at the end of the 1940s, as a copy of the Soviet Russian institutional system—the fruit of pioneering and exemplary Soviet experience. Today it is the dogmatic conviction of the Communist Parties that socialism stands or falls with the preservation intact of this system of institutions, premised on war, with all its sclerotic cumbersomeness.

This institutional system was never either economical or

creative, but as the years went by it became more and more uneconomical and more and more conservative. The population, having gradually learned their way around these burdensome and irrational forms with all their absurd prohibitions against the most self-evident wants, began meanwhile to grow more demanding. In Marxist parlance, the most developed productive forces of all—human beings—are becoming ever more certain that they have outgrown these obsolete relations of production.

At the end of the 1940s the communist leaders justified censorship and police terror on the grounds that this was the royal road to accelerated economic development. Today it is difficult to assert that such measures showed the way to rapid development; on the contrary, they preserved our backwardness. Our state religion and official culture are vestiges of a crabbed war economy.

For nations passing through modernization, it is increasingly difficult to bear the dictatorship of another nation—an experience whose features are unpleasantly familiar from the past of the East Central European societies. Here the weight of empire has retarded on every side the self-determination of society. Here military, dynastic, imperial power has exercised a crippling hegemony over civil society, impeding its development. Here there was too much state and too little society. Modernization was Soviet-type modernization. Agrarian society became urban industrial society by way of Soviet-style institutional forms. Now society's internal dynamics more and more strain the limits of those institutions, which increasingly stifle economic growth, democratic impulses, and aspirations for personal autonomy.

In Hungary a strategy of intelligent accommodation to

the Yalta framework is developing; at the same time, it is a strategy for a more effective loosening of the bonds of Yalta. This strategy deserves to be studied with unbiased attention, for it is being put into practice not just by a government but by a whole society. Demands to try out new reforms are becoming increasingly widespread. Those sectors of the ruling bureaucracy that hoped to make centralized planning more effective through the use of computer technology, replacing brains with bytes, must increasingly face up to the fact that the result is still a wasteful, inflexible, low-efficiency economy. The rule of the Central Committee over the economy leads to indebtedness and chronic shortage. The guardians of the Soviet model are in a difficult fix: the more they cling to it, the more threatening the economic crisis becomes.

Conflicts arise from time to time between the foreign policy framework created at Yalta and the model of society adopted there. Manageable for the most part, at times these conflicts explode. No one can avoid the problem of how to interpret the Yalta framework. The periodic eruption of powerful labor unrest in the Central European countries is a sign of the changes that have taken place. Here and there the working class indicates that it doesn't accept an economic policy which permanently reduces living standards in the name of industrialization, armament, or simply a wasteful centralized planned economy. The planners carry out their muddled notions of hyperindustrialization at the expense of the population, impoverishing society. We have seen something of the kind in Poland and Romania as well. Even within the limits of Yalta there is a better policy than this. In Hungary the power elite is less conceited and more competent, and displays some inherent tendency to develop into a rational bureaucratic elite of professionals. It is broadminded enough to delegate considerable powers of decision (though not in matters of key importance) to lower levels of the power hierarchy. It is gradually disentangling the political and economic spheres, permitting a very slow separation of the various spheres of authority. By decentralizing, it fosters a greater articulation of the whole national economy and thus achieves better results.

In Hungary there is no glaring disparity between the elite's manner of living and that of the bulk of the population. The political bureaucracy allows the technocrats and the other social groups who participate in the second economy to make money—up to a point. The more energetic and resourceful workers can acquire extra income through private avenues, and they don't engage in politics of the traditional working-class sort. Achieving economic independence is their politics.

The communist leadership has achieved—and tolerates—a certain degree of embourgeoisement. By recognizing the right to grumble, it has managed to win over most of the intelligentsia for the national mood of moralizing or academic—and above all, cautious—reformism. It was demonstrated in Hungary in 1956 that cautious opposition intellectuals, lacking any purposeful strategic vision, can suddenly attract broad popular support only in the event of a moral collapse of authority. Only in those circumstances is the bulk of society ready to swing into line behind them. There are times when the moral authority of the state becomes so enfeebled, when its political capital is so depleted, that ad hoc slogans can set the masses in motion and topple the whole state apparatus. The opposition intellectuals wanted something different, but a giant lined up behind them—a flattering but ill-omened surprise.

When there is no actual mass movement; when accommodation to Yalta is calmly proceeding, and along with it the process of relative emancipation from Yalta; when there is none of the bitterness necessary for mass rebellion, because the local elite and the economy it manages are tolerably successful—then it is time to think things through a little more. It is in the opposition's interest that the power elite should function well. It is in the opposition's interest that society should become less polarized and that middle-class development should go on within it, making it less explosion-prone. In a stable society with a tolerant government it is possible to see farther.

It is impossible to alter the Yalta system from inside East Central Europe by means of dynamic, uncontrolled mass movements. That was the lesson of 1956, of 1968, of 1981. It is impossible because the limits of social change are fixed by the military balance, and by a Soviet power elite which labors to preserve the military status quo and has considerable means with which to do it—means that are political as well as military. Some of them are the result of the transplantation of the Soviet model itself—above all, the local political elite, which clings loyally to the imperial structure and arms itself against society.

In extreme cases, the rigid substructure of Yalta itself offers resistance. Soviet military intervention is one form of this. Now another means of implementing Yalta has made its appearance. Armed domestic authority can carry out a

Latin American-style coup against the majority of society.
It is worth remembering that there is a minority in the
state-socialist countries, as everywhere in the world, willing
to go to any extreme to prevent the majority from wresting
power from its hands.

In Hungary the political bureaucracy and the technocracy have worked out an ethos of loose, gradual, whole-
some, unwritten compromise. In so doing, they have made
it difficult for either party to try to step outside the limits of
this ethos. During the past decade the government has left
the opposition intelligentsia at liberty, only subjecting it to
enough unpleasantness to prevent sober people from yearn-
ing to think too much for themselves. It has applied minor
penalties—more on the order of practical everyday restrictions—to make it harder for dissidents to carry out their
activities. It has limited the spread of the opposition subculture through preventive, deterrent police sanctions.

Yet the government has proceeded with more moderation
than the neighboring socialist countries and has induced
intellectuals predisposed to opposition to be more patient.
They have no reason for desperate outbursts, they don't
wish to see a great social movement coalesce around them,
they don't want to steer the country into the storms of
syndicalist upheaval. The Hungarian opposition has more
or less accepted its role of a subculture within the larger
intelligentsia, the function of a cultural and ideological opposition; the kind of soul-searching that springs from the
culture of the workers' movement doesn't appeal to them
very much.

The question is whether in the future the opposition will

be content to remain an intellectual subculture, or whether it will try to become an elite giving impetus and counsel to the workers' movement. Will it want to supply the ideology for a revolutionary workers' movement directed against the ruling state-socialist elite? (Granted that there is no such workers' movement now, nor is it in the intelligentsia's power to create one.)

It is an open question whether martial law would have been introduced in Poland as it was had the Poles not believed that behind the Polish tanks Russian tanks were waiting. Perhaps it would have been done in the same way anyway: there are Soviet-type countries where there are no Soviet troops, only members of the local society who have a stake in seeing the Soviet system remain. It is conceivable that in China, Vietnam, Yugoslavia, or Cuba armed authority might have responded in the same way, if society had launched a radical effort toward emancipation and attempted to conquer democratic rights by means of a revolutionary mass movement. There are Soviet-type subelites that readily fit into the institutional structure of Yalta.

No such radical movement of emancipation has ever occurred in a Soviet-type country that was not under Soviet occupation. China, North Korea, Vietnam, Laos, Cambodia, Mongolia, Romania, Yugoslavia, Albania, South Yemen, Mozambique, Ethiopia, Angola, Cuba—in these fourteen countries, no one has ever tried with any prospect of success to overthrow the rule of a Soviet-type elite. In none of these countries has society been able to rise up against the state.

In Europe, the Soviet model has no great appeal. No communist dictatorship has ever been born here without Soviet assistance. On the other side of the Iron Curtain, the fascist-type dictatorships have melted away. They proved inadequate to the task of organizing society and to the demands of growing national integration. Spain, Portugal, and Greece under their respective juntas became too complex for the dictatorial state to go on stifling their internal stirrings any longer or shut their people off from the currents of the larger world.

We must have confidence in this growing complexity—in the fact that a society can gradually slough off dictatorship, and that the prime mover in that process is a growing middle class. Proletarian revolution didn't break out in any country of southern Europe. If it had, the military dictatorships would only have hardened. The middle class, on the other hand, imperceptibly swallowed up the rough-hewn military structures.

The forces shifted within the elites as they came to see that their interests were better served by forms of government other than dictatorship. This is what we were hoping for, and this is what we must encourage in the Eastern European elites, even in the power elites, so that they themselves will want to bid farewell to dictatorship. The Soviet model cannot be exported to relatively developed countries without generating, before long, serious pressures in society for reform of the model itself.

The road we have to travel goes by way of the articulation and consolidation of the East Central European societies on a European model. We need to enrich our experience of how the two independent variables—Warsaw Pact membership and one-party rule—can be brought into more diverse and more flexible relationship with the dependent variables that are only relatively determined by them. How can we develop into ever stronger independent variables our Central European situation, our national past, our belated embourgeoisement, the consolidation of our intellectual middle class and its functional cooperation with the working class (especially the elite of better educated and more enterprising workers), and the gradual withdrawal of censorship from the channels of communication and from public consciousness?

How, then, can we make the social status quo more of an independent variable with respect to the military status quo? How can we strengthen the horizontal human relationships of civil society against the vertical human relationships of military society? How can a society adapt to those two fixed facts—the Soviet alliance and the one-party system—in such a way that in every other sphere of life it can display the greatest autonomy: the freedom to express its own individuality, while at the same time cultivating its share of the common European consciousness?

This strategy is not an unequivocally enjoyable one. It is a Sisyphean task to toil at the gradual lifting of restrictions which would only be ridiculed elsewhere, to analyze for rational content dogmas which would simply be impossible elsewhere in the context of European rationalism. The fact that only a Party member can be a leader, or that an idea can appear only if acceptable to the Party—these are archaic requirements; it's as if the bourgeois revolutions carried through elsewhere centuries ago had never reached our frontiers. Human rights, a matter of common consensus in Europe, are still a dream for us, and bold, persistent work will be needed before they are really ours.

We cannot expect them from others, not from the Russians or the Americans or the Western Europeans. To complain about this is childish. There is no exemption from the general rule that every people has to conquer its own freedom. Even if there were, many internal convulsions are still necessary before a nation can free itself from the vestiges of predemocratic authoritarianism and servility. It is up to us Eastern Europeans to hammer out for ourselves the democratic rights whose exercise long ago became second nature in Western Europe.

The goal—freedom—is absolute; the road that leads to it is relative. It is each and every individual's personal road. It leads through a network of communities, linked with one another by ties of spiritual sympathy.

SOCIETY WITH A STRATEGY: STRONGER THAN THE ARMED STATE

Our great dream: what would it be like if the Russian politburo were like the English queen? Our dependence would give way eventually to a community of interests, and in the meantime the politburo would become more and more symbolic. The subject nations would express their devotion ceremonially and from afar, and the crown would accept this as sufficient.

For that to happen, Moscow would have to become a center of civilization capable of offering its partners more than obsolete technology and dependent, top-down forms of communication. When the colonizer is no more advanced economically and culturally than the colonized, it becomes necessary to draw up the weapons again and again as a sure argument for the perpetuation of dependence.

To be sure, it is no easy matter to transform this kind of relationship into an internationalism of equal partners. Moscow has not carried out its own reform; it consistently subordinates its consumer industry to military production, and so its wares are far less well represented on the Eastern European consumer and cultural market than they might be. Thus it is unable to attract our societies with its goods and fashions and so win them over from within.

We can learn to love the Russians in the films of Tarkovsky and Mikhalkov, but the visits of the tanks and the marshals seldom stir warmth in the hearts of Hungarians, Czechs, and Poles. If Hungarian tourists could drive around in the Soviet Union, roaming wherever they wished; if they could eat in inexpensive restaurants, find bargains in Soviet shops, and make friends with frank and open Soviet citizens; if the Soviet artistic avant-garde occupied a prominent place in the world of the arts; if it were worth learning Russian because you could learn something about the world from Russian newspapers; if Hungarians returned from their visits feeling they had seen an interesting and expressive society—then fraternal sentiments would be aroused spontaneously and the unpleasant memory of two suppressed revolutions (1849 and 1956) would fade before the realization that here is a neighbor worth visiting.

Reformist allies could deal more easily with a reformist Soviet leadership; they would enjoy more autonomy in their relations with it. We have the most fundamental interest in Soviet reform. We cannot create a life truly worthy of human beings for ourselves so long as our neighbors do not undertake to create the same for themselves. With a reformist Soviet Union, we could reinterpret our relationship with more detachment, refining it into genuine friendship.

The greatest obstacle to friendly feelings toward the Soviet Union is the Soviet Union itself, insofar as it behaves like an inflexible and frightening power. There would be friendship for the Soviet Union in Eastern Europe if only the Soviets wouldn't lecture and scold; if they didn't grow suspicious at every sign of spontaneity; if their official culture didn't speak querulously and condescendingly; if they weren't so firmly convinced that they are unique, the first in everything (which only reveals how little they know of the world); if Russian culture weren't such a closed culture, meanly censoring foreign influences—for then there would be reason for us to be friends.

As it is, there is more reason for us to be fearful, and the more fearful we are, the less we can be friends. Even the warmest collaborators cannot make themselves believe that the tanks which blow our cities to pieces can evoke tender sentiments in our hearts. Furthermore, there are Hungarians living in the Soviet Union, in areas that belonged to Hungary for a thousand years, who live less well than we do. They would like to migrate, but it's very difficult for them to do so.

If we are not equals, no friendship is possible. The Soviet Union encounters friendlier feelings in Finland than in Poland, Czechoslovakia, or Hungary, precisely because peo-

ple are the friendliest where the Soviet Union has caused
them the least suffering. There isn't a single Hungarian
family today that hasn't suffered injury, inconvenience, or
loss because of the Russian system.

In Hungary a great effect was produced by the charming
little story about the ambassador of the Mongolian People's
Republic who, in his first official note after taking up his
duties here, apologized in the name of his government for
Genghis Khan's cruel invasion of 1241, which half destroyed
our country.

The historical memory of a nation is the personal memory of its people; our fathers' memories are our own. Oppression's most powerful enemy is the memory of the sur-
vivors and their descendants. We Hungarians have long felt
ashamed because we occupied part of the Ukraine for two or
three years during World War II. Now *they* ought to start
being ashamed for having kept us under occupation for
nearly forty years.

We cannot be free, of course, so long as we cannot decide
our own destinies—so long as we cannot vote another party
into office for a few years, if we wish, instead of the Communist Party. Then we would see if people would still
choose the Communist Party! So long as a party leadership
is not dependent on us because we can vote it down, we are
dependent on it because it can send us up. So long as the
Party doesn't need to court the people's favor, it will spend
a great deal on the police and the army; our cities will
remain neglected, and we will walk down the street with
our heads hunched between our shoulders.

The a priori leading role of the party and the a priori
fidelity to the Soviet alliance are both unnatural. Force, lies,

and fear are needed to maintain them. The people know that elsewhere it's worse. They know that our cities will be overrun by Soviet armies if we overthrow Party rule and leave the Warsaw Pact, so they cast their lot with a milder tyranny in preference to a more brutal one. The population supports the existing government because they know it's the only one they're going to get, but they want to induce it to be a little nicer. The population suspects that perhaps the leaders, too, do what they do because they have to. We all do what we have to do, for lack of anything better. We are comrades in misfortune. We suspect that our leaders don't worship the central controllers either, because we ourselves don't worship central controllers of any kind. For that reason, we expect mutual respect from each other.

We have to test the flexibility of those elements of the system which have not been declared axiomatic. We ought to regard the Communist Party as a party that has just won 51 percent of the vote in parliamentary elections. After a few more elections it will probably receive a solid majority consistently. At that point, it will be possible for a minority to exist, equipped with the requisite basic human rights. The actual majority ought to act as if it were a minority. Very well, we will act that way. We will not call the legitimacy of the regime into question by turning to illegitimate methods. We want only to make the point that we know what we know and that we are neither blind nor feeble-minded.

Everyone who says what he thinks speaks from the hearts of the listening majority. Speaking as one of those who are kept within bounds rather than as one of those who keep them there, I'd say the regime was making a great mistake if it believed the 98 percent approval it receives in single-list elections. I wouldn't think it could pursue a rational policy on the basis of such a belief.

The regime would do well not to abuse its power, so loyally acknowledged. We ask it to exercise that power in civilized fashion, with all due modesty. Let it be dignified, good-humored, and respectful toward everyone it deals with at home and abroad, the strong and the weak, Westerners and Easterners, friends and critics alike. We would like a government with a sense of style. If as a result of Yalta we must have a conservative government, let it compensate by reviving the finest traditions of the Austro-Hungarian monarchy's liberalism, which also paraded under a cloak of conservative paternalism. If the Party must tower over us like the monarchy, let the court life be glittering and the court aristocracy magnanimous.

If the democratic masses can no longer raise demagogues to high authority, if the state no longer needs to fear the passions of the crowd, if the politicians can now exercise power with aristocratic continuity, like feudal lords, then let the state be really rational and stop insisting on political reliability rather than knowledge and ability.

In the leadership positions everyone is reliable anyway, as a matter of national strategy. On the whole, we know what can be done in any given position. We know what the leaders can do—both those in office and those who have been thrown out of office. This is the permanent division of roles in the Eastern European play; the casting has a centuries-old history. Not everyone needs a speaking part, of course, but someone has to speak. On our greatest national holiday

we walk to the statue of a poet* who on that day more than
a century and a quarter ago printed a poem, without permission from the censor.

Our legally licensed political culture has to act as if loyalty to our alliance and to exclusive Communist Party rule
were the honorable, obvious, and indispensable basis of our
existence. No honest author would so much as stray into the
vicinity of these two idols. I would rather not feel the sense
of triumph that fills the honest licensed writer when he
succeeds in adroitly avoiding this pair of taboos. They have
elevated avoidance almost to the level of an aesthetic.

The temptation to simply let our minds consider whatever appeals to us is understandable. Those who say what
they think are like students in a conservative school who
have had their first experience of physical love. Like anti-
bodies to the censorship bodies, we can say from experience
that we have chosen what is good for us. Our censors envy
us; they too would like to say what they think. I am an
optimist because I know that desire is bolder than fear. The
good cheer of the people will overcome their fear of the
state. Let every underling find ways to soften up his superior. I am confident that the tension in the ranks of the
powerful is relenting, and that the executive intelligentsia
is ready to enter into open dialogue with the creative intelligentsia.

And we—Hungarian intellectuals who try to think more

---

* Sándor Petőfi (1823–49), who played an active role in the Hungarian revolution of 1848–49 and whose patriotic songs gained him the reputation of
Hungary's national poet. [Publisher's note.]

or less independently—what are we to do? We should try to influence other intellectuals and those who wield power, who are obliged by the demands of their jobs to impose a greater censorship on themselves. Self-censorship is painful, because increased tension and aggressiveness go with it. Those who censor themselves less ought to tempt those who censor themselves more. We ought to encourage the internal emancipation of all those whom we meet. Self-censorship builds the state's paranoia into our own personalities. Those who choose to think for themselves are hedonists. It is better to laugh with dissidents than with members of the governing party.

The greatest act on behalf of freedom is to behave toward everyone as though we were free men—even toward those whom we fear. If we act that way with them, they will think we are not really afraid of them.

We have to be oppositionists in order to be fair toward those in power. I have noticed that cautious people speak more harshly of our political leaders than the outsiders do. Civil society is still only an idea; let us look at ourselves here in Budapest as if from the island of Utopia.

WHAT DOES THE WEST WANT: TO DRIVE THE RUSSIAN ELITE INTO A CORNER OR TO HELP IT REFORM?

We must also think through our situation from what we take to be the viewpoint of the Soviet ruling elite. Is there any possible alternative policy for them that doesn't threaten a radical disruption of our ties (or even the whole empire), but that would differ from current policy, whose essence is a costly and dangerous arms buildup?

Eastern Europe tried to draw closer to the West by importing its technology on credit and is now in debt up to its ears. The more centralized a state economy, the more recklessly it makes use of loans, and the more painfully it squeezes the population to reduce their standard of living in order to pay the price of senseless waste. It now appears that there are political limits to the capacity of communist economies to heap up catastrophes.

Our lack of creditworthiness is making a shambles of East-West economic ties. The possibility exists of a new autarchy within our camp and within each country. In Moscow they may well think they have to hang on to Hungary, Czechoslovakia, and Poland at all cost, because if these countries break away, the Ukraine will be next. Another period of anti-Western isolation could lead to a neoslavophile autocracy, this time under military rather than Party auspices.

Is a moderate, authoritarian reform possible on an empire-wide scale—an enlightened Party monarchy, a "Hungarian" style of exercising power? How—except through the threat of revolutionary terror—can a ruling elite shake up the power structure without risking the loss of power itself? The Russian elite wants their regime to survive, to function, and to enjoy respect in the world, without war. We who are dependent on them want the Russian elite to be spared having to govern in a state of panic.

The fundamental question—to which any revolutionary would answer with a sarcastic "no"—is: can an ossified, conservative elite absorb ideas that are foreign to it? Can it distribute and devolve power so as to exercise it more skillfully, so that the danger of collapse will no longer threaten it? Our not altogether reassuring experience has been that communism will break before it will bend.

In the West, many would like to see a spectacular internal collapse of the Soviet empire. They believe that the West would not be endangered by such a collapse. I consider this belief naive. Russian leaders have traditionally warded off collapse by externalizing domestic conflicts. When they are unbending at home they are also unbending abroad. At such times they are less open to negotiations and produce external challenges one after the other. The more critical the situation becomes, the more they militarize.

Would a humiliated and enfeebled Soviet elite cooperate against their will in the dismantling of the empire? It would be foolish to expect anything of the kind. I have observed that they defend themselves vigorously: they strike hard, though no harder than necessary. Their actions are purposeful, aimed at consolidating their power; it cannot be said they behave irrationally. The rationale they follow is not so good for us, however. We think there are other possibilities that are better for them as well.

Since we are shut up together in one camp anyway, we ought to exchange our views sincerely. Thinking people in Eastern Europe should engage in an open exchange of ideas with thinking people in the Soviet Union. There are some, both here and there. It cannot be said that theirs are the dominant voices, but they don't go completely unheard either. We must persuade the Russian elite to care more about improving their leadership style and to examine the way they exercise power, in a more realistic and demanding light.

Perhaps the most intriguing question of all is: how would it be possible to smooth the way intellectually for some kind of permanent reconciliation of interests between the American and Russian elites? How can the potential negotiating partners be freed from the grip of ideology and demonology? How can the Western elite gain some influence over developments taking place within the Eastern elite?

Here the basic question is, what is the objective of Western strategy? If it looks to a collapse, the strategy is mistaken —there won't be any collapse. There won't, because a collapse would be too dangerous, too frightening—because the West doesn't want to fight: it would rather buy its security. It would rather pay, just as long as the other side doesn't lose its head.

The West would also pay to draw the Soviet bloc into the world market, even without the threat that the bloc might slip into social and economic crisis because it is so poorly integrated into the world market. In the post-Stalin era, Eastern strategy has been to enter the world market gradually, to produce for export with technology bought with Western credits, while at the same time keeping central direction intact and rejecting basic, liberalizing structural reforms. This strategy is exhausted. Now it is a matter of either reform or a crisis of indebtedness.

Western creditors have an interest in placing their money sensibly, in investments that pay; otherwise, they will not get their return. They ought to extend credit, but on very specific terms, and only after assuring themselves that the borrower has the capacity to repay the debt. If the borrower doesn't initiate reform, he will not be able to pay. The Polish and Romanian governments squandered their Western credits and are now trying to repay them with exports of foodstuffs, while their own people stand in line in front of the food shops. Is that in the interest of the Western creditors?

Credits from the West are in the best interest of the people of Eastern Europe, but only if the creditors are convinced that their money will be spent rationally in the civilian economy. The more closely the Eastern civilian economy is linked to the world market, the easier it becomes to link it more closely still. Beyond a certain threshold, an export-sensitive state economy has to be liberalized. An era has ended: now it is either withdrawal again, or a new and more successful opening. In the Soviet bloc there is only one way to an opening: the Hungarian way. Can this experience be extended to the bloc as a whole?

Western economic strategy and the Eastern European reform intelligentsia can work together to give the Eastern European and Soviet elite a stake in liberalization. Can the elite's position be made both flexible and secure?

It is the labor of a lifetime to induce the imperial center to carry out economic reform, to give the empire a stake in embourgeoisement. Credits shouldn't be denied, but they shouldn't be given blindly either. Refusal to give creditors a voice in the use of the funds, on the basis of national or state pride, is unacceptable. It's not popular sovereignty that would be infringed by giving them oversight over their investments, but rather the sovereignty of the decision-making oligarchy. Let the oligarchy be overseen at least from without, if it cannot be overseen from below. Aid should be given for civilian—not military—purposes, to develop agricultural technology and consumer industry; it should be given in exchange for economic reforms and respecting human rights. It would be fitting if credit-worthiness were reduced in proportion to the number of political arrests.

The West will get further with a shrewd external economic policy than with the pressure of an arms race. The latter is obviously more expensive as well. The fact that the West has chosen the more expensive and less effective strategy indicates that the Western elite is also the captive of its own ideology.

In Eastern Europe, nevertheless, there is no silencing antistatist criticism, which has demonstrated that state autocracy serves only the interests of the state oligarchy, while the majority of the population loses by it. Antistatist criticism cannot be stilled any more than anticapitalist criticism, which has demonstrated again and again that capitalism is a system fraught with conflicts and inequities.

Soviet-type communism assures neither the rule of the majority nor the rights of minorities. Instead, it places the interests of the state first, along with the interests of the bloc, organized on a military basis; these have an unequivocal priority over the rights of human beings. This system is the continuation of an Eastern tradition that placed imperial organization above human rights. Such was the Chinese Empire, such was the Ottoman Empire, and such was its immediate predecessor, the Russian Empire of the czars.

The thinking of the Russian elite straddles two value systems. One is the Western, Christian, European, pluralist, rationalist system of values; the other is an Asiatic, autocratic, imperial, dogmatic value system, fanatically suspicious in the face of change. These two value systems have waged a dramatic struggle more than once in the Russian soul, and it can scarcely be said that the contest has been decided in favor of one or the other. From time to time it appears that the Western appeal has faded, but then new Westernizers appear, reviving the fundamental paradox of the Russian psyche, which is to be European by Asiatic standards and Asiatic by European standards. At present, it appears, the dogmatic, imperial element has gained the upper hand. There is no way, however, for the middle-class intelligentsia to give up altogether representing Western values within the empire.

We are faced with a Eurasian power, a strong and numerous people tempted by the challenging prospect of Eurasian hegemony. To this day the Russian elite has not been able to decide which of the two value systems to choose, because their antinomy is rooted in the elite's historical reality and the elite cannot exist without either one. It would be absurd to give up on the Russians as creative partners, as if they were subjects of some Asiatic despotism, but it would be equally absurd to demand that they convert to the values of Atlantic civilization. The Russians will never be unequivocally Asiatic or unequivocally European. At most they will place greater emphasis on the one or the other. Ever since Tolstoy and Dostoyevsky, a firmly rooted tradition has held that they have gained something by not being completely European. The West must come to terms with what is most authentically Russian.

While the Western European colonial empires have evaporated, giving way to independent political entities, the Russian colonial empire, already swollen to huge proportions by czarist expansion, has been preserved and even enlarged by the Soviet leadership. And by reason of its military weight and single-minded strategy, it is bound to grow still more in the interests of stability itself. The imperial elite has understood that calling a halt means decay and that growth is essential to survival. This elite is unquestionably proud of having created, with the help of Soviet ideology, a uniform modern civilization over enormous, ethnically diverse areas where for the most part precapitalist economic structures existed before.

It is a fact that both pre- and postrevolutionary Russian expansion contributed lastingly to this process. And it is possible to argue that the Moslem peoples of the Soviet Union (for example) live better than do their Moslem relatives in Asia south of the Soviet frontier. But the same cannot be said of the East Germans by comparison with the West Germans, which indicates the special character of the European scene.

It was East Central Europe's historical misfortune that it was unable to become independent after the collapse of the Eastern, Tartar-Turkish hegemony and later the German-Austrian hegemony of the West, and that it once again came under Eastern hegemony, this time of the Soviet Russian type. This is what prevents our area from exercising the Western option taken out a thousand years ago, even though that represents our profoundest historical inclinations.

It would be in our best interest to escape this imperial

tutelage, to become independent and neutral states. We
have learned that it is impossible to persuade the Russian
elite to dissolve itself or to stand passively by while the empire dissolves. Nor is it possible to fool them; we cannot act
as if the issue were something other than our wish for
greater independence from them: that is what we want; that
is what we have to talk about.

To compel the Russian elite, equipped as it is with weapons that can assure nuclear annihilation many times over, to
withdraw its military control over certain areas is an impossibility. Those who say it is possible are demagogues. What
is possible at most is to make a deal with the Soviet leadership.

I know the West doesn't want to redeem us. It prefers to
shake its head over us, and sometimes it pays its regrets. I
know that in fact neither the Russians nor the Americans
nor even the Western Europeans really care about Yalta—
we East Central Europeans alone care. So I speak from anything but a disinterested point of view. I would like to
persuade everyone at least to begin work on the peaceful
demolition of the Yalta edifice, because otherwise we East
Central Europeans will never be free. My thesis is that this
goal is in the basic interest of all the affected parties because
the Yalta system ineluctably gives rise to the danger of a
third world war, a danger that is constantly growing. I
would like to show that our liberation is a life-and-death
concern for both Russians and Westerners.

These are difficult goods to sell, an expert in ideological
marketing might say. Indeed, one look at the Russian elite
is enough to tell you it's a tough nut to crack. We see there a

deeply rooted mistrust, a habit of viewing the opposition as agents of the enemy, of externalizing conflicts, of perceiving anything that brings elements of heterogeneity into the system as the sinister inroads of an external foe. Clinging to a mistrust and a nationalism that preserve power and foster expansion is hardly a new phenomenon in the history of the Russian elite.

The empire cannot be pushed back, thinks the West, nor will it advance any farther. We are not going any farther west, think the Russians, but we are not going to pull back, either. Meanwhile we Hungarians, Czechs, and Poles huddle here on the western margin of the empire and on the eastern side of the Iron Curtain, with a cautious strategy of limited self-preservation and a troubled mind, because we don't want to identify with the East and we can't identify with the West.

ANTIPOLITICS: A MORAL FORCE

The political leadership elites of our world don't all subscribe equally to the philosophy of a nuclear *ultima ratio*, but they have no conceptual alternative to it. They have none because they are professionals of power. Why should they choose values that are in direct opposition to physical force? Is there, can there be, a political philosophy—a set of proposals for winning and holding power—that renounces a priori any physical guarantees of power? Only antipolitics offers a radical alternative to the philosophy of a nuclear *ultima ratio*.

Antipolitics strives to put politics in its place and make sure it stays there, never overstepping its proper office of defending and refining the rules of the game of civil society. Antipolitics is the ethos of civil society, and civil society is the antithesis of military society. There are more or less militarized societies—societies under the sway of nation-states whose officials consider total war one of the possible moves in the game. Thus military society is the reality, civil society is a utopia.

Antipolitics means refusing to consider nuclear war a satisfactory answer in any way. Antipolitics regards it as impossible in principle that any historical misfortune could be worse than the death of one to two billion people. Antipolitics bases politics on the conscious fear of death. It recognizes that we are a homicidal and suicidal species, capable of thinking up innumerable moral explanations to justify our homicidal and suicidal tendencies.

We shouldn't shy away from the suspicion that the generals think of war with something other than pure horror. It's inconceivable that the American President or the Russian President is not pleased at the thought of being the most powerful man in the world. His pleasure is only disturbed, perhaps, by the fact that he can't be quite sure about it, since his opposite number may very well think the same thing.

A politician is better, the more power he has. Politicians who don't love power or don't love it enough are not the norm. Destiny punishes their dilettantism by not giving them very much power and not for very long.

Picture the faces of Stalin and Brezhnev, Mao Tse-tung and Deng Hsiao-ping, Tito and Franco, Adenauer and de Gaulle: on each there is a shrewd and forceful sensualism that imposes itself on its surroundings. Their mathematical or psychological acumen may have been only average, but their power skills were certainly above average. Their talent for power should be measured not by anything they said but by how long they managed to hang on to leadership positions ardently desired by others.

Women loved Don Juan because he loved them, ardently and energetically, as a matter of life and death. Augustus became a god-emperor because he loved power, ardently and energetically, as a matter of life and death. Hardy elder statesmen and heads of government make us feel that politics—like economics, art, or love—is an independent sphere of existence not translatable into any other language, not reducible to any other dimension.

Politics cannot be explained in any context or medium but its own—the rich network of relationships that we call power. Politicians may have to reckon with economic interests, cultural conventions, and religious passions, but politics itself cannot be derived from economics, culture, or religion. Any approach to politics is bound to fail if it strays far from the standpoint of that political genius Machiavelli, who explained power by saying that power wills itself and that the prince wants not only to gain power but also to keep and enlarge it. That's his function—his obligation, if you like. Any philosophy of history will miss its mark if it tries to explain the riddle of political power in terms of economic interest, biological instinct, or religious enthusiasm.

For politics, anything that is not politics is merely an instrument, not a reason or a goal. If we don't reduce mysticism or money-making to something else, if we don't believe that a great painter paints because it's the way to God or riches, then why should we think that the great born politicians want power for some ulterior reason, good or bad, rather than for the sake of power itself? It's just as natural for them to love power as it is for a champion skier to love the slopes and the snow. Since humanity is hypocritical (and public opinion is particularly so), they have to pretend they love something more inspiring—their country, for example. If they succeed in making the public believe it, they are good politicians and deserve their power.

For the rest of us who are not politicians, the less power a politician has, the better—the less we have to fear from him. I find Austrian and Hungarian politicians more reassuring than Russian or American politicians, for example, because they are a menace to fewer people. If Austria and Hungary should go to war—in itself a ridiculous notion in this day and age—humanity would have little to fear. But if the Russian and American leaders should go to war—in itself a far from ridiculous notion—then the whole world and all humanity would have a great deal to fear indeed.

I hardly think it would be easy to deprive the Russian and American politicians of their technical capacity to kill one to two billion people. It's possible that they will not make use of this potential, but they still insist on having the theoretical capability so they can use it in a situation where they deem it necessary. These are men who can imagine a situation where there is nothing else to do but order the launching of nuclear weapons, where it would be right and proper to kill one or two billion people! Both political elites see nuclear escalation as right and proper in the event that either one should try to take power away from the other. This mentality is a functional characteristic of the leaders of the nuclear powers.

The career of Adolf Hitler was an extreme paradigm of the politician's trade. He rose from the ranks of the feckless lumpen-intelligentsia to become Götterdämmerung incarnate over the bodies of fifty million people, like a wayside angel of death. When he addressed his followers, a veritable frenzy of verbal aggression gripped the speaker himself and suffused the glowing faces of his listeners as they breathed "Sieg Heil!" in response.

I am afraid of a third world war because, to my mind, there lives in every politician more or less of the delirium that was Hitler's demon. More exalted than the others, he could find exhilaration in pure unbridled power abstracted from all other considerations, from economic rationality or cultural values. We have to be wary of them because in all politicians worth their salt there is present, albeit in more sober form, some of the dynamite that came out in Hitler with such savage brutality; if there were not, they would not have chosen the politician's trade.

No matter what ideology a politician may appeal to, what he says is only a means of gaining and keeping power. A politician for whom the exercise of power is not an end in itself is a contradiction in terms. In culturally stable societies this kind of cynicism runs up against strong social and ethical inhibitions, and any observer who discerns this cynicism behind the inhibitions is himself called cynical. In less well-balanced societies the relentless instrumentalism of political power may come to the fore in hysterical crises of identity, exacerbating hidden suicidal tendencies by hazarding the greatest risk of all, the doomsday gamble.

Politicians have to be guarded against because the peculiarity of their function and mentality lies in the fact that they are at times capable of pushing the button for atomic war. There is in them some of that mysterious hubris that would like to elevate the frail and mortal "I" into a simulacrum of the Almighty. If this psychic dynamite should go off, it could draw all mankind into a global Auschwitz.

Why should I as a writer stick my nose into political matters? Because they frighten me. I feel mortally threatened by them, because there is more and more talk in political circles of rearmament and the likelihood of war. If the other side doesn't back down, they say, there will be war, and the responsibility will be wholly theirs.

All right, I look at the other side: they don't back down, and they say exactly the same thing. All right, I say, neither one will back down, now what? Are they going to have it out, or are they bluffing? Are they just trying to scare us, or are they serious after all?

I am speaking out because I feel confined by the Iron Curtain and the web of censorship restrictions that has grown up along with it. I know I may be locked up if tensions mount and the regime becomes more stringent. Most of the world is poor and military waste infuriates me. I loathe a culture that represents preparations to kill millions of people as a patriotic obligation. Thanks to the whims of politicians, I have more than once been in a fair way to depart violently from this scene, where otherwise it is still possible to live a good life. On the basis of their public statements, I suspect that politicians still think of war, even in the nuclear age, as a possible political action—"politics with bloodshed," to quote Mao Tse-tung's more graphic version of Clausewitz's aphorism.

I don't like it when they want to kill me. I don't like it when the agents of the politicians hold a gun on me. To me it doesn't matter much whether a bomb kills me or a death squad. To die by war is no better than to die by terror. War is terror too; the possibility of war is terror, and those who prepare for war are terrorists. The prospect of war and the absence of democracy are two sides of the same reality: politicians threatening defenseless people. If reality means people working at their own deaths for fatuous reasons, then I am bound to think reality even more absurd than deadly.

Escalation is the rule when weapons are put to use, yet no manner of social conflict can be solved by atom bombs. Our entire mythology of revolution and counterrevolution is an anachronistic shadow from the days of simple firearms. I am convinced that the redeeming doctrine of war as a continuation of power politics—the doctrine of the balance of terror —doesn't work any longer.

The abject stupidity of the flower of our intellectuals has contributed to the killing of millions in the big and little wars of this century. The ideologue is responsible because it is possible to kill with ideologies. In order to make war, drop bombs, build concentration camps, and dispose efficiently of the bodies, the skills of intellectuals are required.

I am repelled by men of ideas who chatter in tune with the military's propaganda machinery, who never lifted a finger against the butchery, who are left with only the sad excuse of declaring afterward that they were not in agreement with the terror to which they paid homage. A disturbingly large proportion of our thinkers have become experts in the service of our leaders. They are at pains to depict in rational colors something that is deathly irrational. The intellectual specialists in the logic of atomic and ideological war get their money for deceiving others, for leading them like lambs to the slaughter.

I was in a slaughterhouse once—I saw the lambs. A sly-faced black ram led them. Just before reaching the block he slipped to one side, escaping from that corridor of death through a trapdoor. The others, following in his tracks, kept on going—right up to the block. They called the black ram Miska. After each of these performances he would go up to the canteen, where he was given a roll with salami and some cake, and he would eat. For me, the scholars of ideological war are so many Miskas, except that they themselves have no way of slipping through any trapdoor to safety.

WAR AND PEACE: NOT FOR A POLITICIAN TO DECIDE

The question of peace and war between East and West is first and foremost a historical and philosophical question, and only secondarily a military and foreign-policy one. There is no need to demonstrate that it is a question which touches us all. In matters that affect everyone there is no historical or philosophical justification for one group of bureaucratic authorities and their experts—the political class—to make the decisions, excluding the rest of us from any right to decide or to discuss the decision, since there is absolutely no guarantee that the government is any better equipped to take the right stand on any historic issue than thinking people who don't hold government office. And from the standpoint of democracy it is no more legitimate, because decisions of war and peace are too serious to be delegated through representation to a political elite. They are matters for popular referendum, at the very least; the usual delegation of political authority, which confers the right to conduct routine state affairs, is insufficient here.

A politician rises to the highest office in the two super-powers either through multiparty elections or bureaucratic selection. His intellectual capacity, to judge from a quick survey of Soviet and American leaders since the last war, is no greater than that of the average person. As a matter of principle, his judgment cannot be competent to decide, in our stead, about our life or death. Incommensurable values stand in opposition here: on one side, the consistent sovereignty of the state; on the other, the life or death of all or nearly all of its people. Who could blame the people for thinking the state's sovereignty less important than their own lives? Especially since we have a new relationship to war today: before, people could believe that they would survive individually, but today they cannot even believe that.

Looking back on the wars of the past, weighing retrospectively the actions of statesmen, we see clearly that they might have decided differently. They made errors of judgment. Their prejudices led them to miscalculate. Those prejudices sprang from the characteristic ideologies of their time, which posterity looks upon with amazement. The powerful—and the intellectuals who spoke in one voice with them—became entangled in a web of their era's prevailing misjudgments. Looking back afterward, even schoolboys can see that. When it comes to the present, however, even university professors forget it.

How pathetic the old kings and statesmen were, princes of broken empires! Their pride, their pomp, their arrogance were all founded on the illusion that their power could grow larger still, could even become all-powerful.

We see the political leaders of earlier times falling victim to the spell of power, almost as if it were a clinical illness. We see how sane and sober men became paranoiacs, megalomaniacs, possessed beings who would listen to no one. We see how the possession of power turned into a sickness—so much so that we must regard power itself as a pathogenic factor. Those who suffer from power are inclined to suffer from the sickness of self-inflation, the boundless overreaching of the ego.

For that reason political power, as an institution, ought to be surrounded with extraordinary suspicion, with precautionary measures, and with the most stringent vigilance that civil society can muster. For those who possess it are swept by an insatiable passion for more, and are tempted to vie with others who have it, until they come to think of history as only a poker game of kings and presidents in which people are no more than the playing cards.

To Kill or Not to Kill?

"Thou shalt not kill" is the religious person's strongest prohibition. If I knew who was going to die I would also know that every time it is someone who is, in the nature of things, incomparable. Everyone who has a mother knows that every old woman is incomparable.

Man is appalled at his own powers: he can release forces that will kill indiscriminately. To me it seems that there must be some profound darkness in the mind of anyone who kills. I understand why the people's courts are more indulgent in cases of murder committed in anger, jealousy, or self-defense; the transports of passion are temporary. But the permanent, armed, rational intention to kill is something else again; we are right to be appalled by it.

I would really be hard put to say whether, from a religious standpoint, there is any difference between a general and a war criminal. We cannot regard the general as unaccountable: he knows what he's doing. Perhaps he has already killed before; in any event, he is planning to kill now.

My destiny is more powerful than I am and so perhaps I will kill, but if that misfortune should befall me, I would have the right to commit suicide afterward, and, in so doing, I would execute a murderer. I don't claim that anyone else would have the right to kill me: my homicide doesn't justify yours. But anyone would have a right to come look me in the eye and say, "Murderer!"

Anyone should be free to call me by my proper name. I couldn't charge anyone with slander for calling me that, not even another murderer. Someone else might come look me in the eye and never say anything. She might give me something to eat, she might make love with me, but to the murderer she wouldn't say a word.

We are capable of killing one another and we are capable of not killing one another; indeed, we are capable of loving one another. Which we will do is not laid down in our instincts. This perilous freedom is the essence of the human drama.

Shouldn't every human being reflect on whether he would or would not kill his neighbor for one reason or another? Sometimes a trifle is enough for some to give a positive answer—for example, a gold tooth that can be knocked from a jaw. We also have the power to kill the neighbor closest to us—ourselves. We know this victim close at hand: suicide is the absolute murder. A third world war would be humanity's absolute crime.

One person's consciousness cannot substitute for another's, since the other person's life has been different. My history differs from everyone else's. How ridiculously little it is to say of anyone that he was wise, or pious, or a scoundrel, or a killer. There are no words of this sort that would sum up my nature in its entirety. If there is truth in the assertion that God is always greater—*Deus semper maior*—then there is also truth in the assertion that man is always greater. For that reason we cannot make any higher moral demand on ourselves than to respect and honor this greaterness, and if possible not to kill it.

History, on the other hand, consists of nothing but mutual killing, robbing, deceit, and humiliation; that's the stuff of history. It is a record of the slyest possible commission of acts that religion and culture consider criminal. Pious talk and crimes to match—that's the kind of hypocrisy that history speaks of.

But is crime the only thing that has happened? It is true that in our chronicles we commemorate wickedness; perhaps we do so because it's relatively uncommon. In a certain village the women often nurse their children, but they very seldom strangle them. History takes no note when a woman feeds her family. Love is more common than murder, peace is more common than war. Men beat their wives, but that's the exception; more often, they kiss them.

Goodness is all around us, as unnoticed as the earth and the air. Our human reality is woven of cooperation, and violence is the rip in the fabric. But the rip is still not the most important characteristic of the fabric. Peace is stronger than war because the weight of everyday life is on its side. The memorable life collected in the chronicles isn't all crime either; there is resistance to crime as well—sometimes, to be sure, by fighting fire with fire, with lesser crimes such as thoughtlessness or neglect, which can be fatal, too.

While man, as a species, is capable of suicide, the everyday life of individuals gives us reassurance that our species will confront this absolute crime and will not commit it. When evil stands at the door, we have to open the door and look it in the eye. If we ignore it or try to hide, it will break down the door upon us.

The Utopia of World Socialism and the Absence of Peace

Who is to make the ultimate philosophical, ideological, strategic, and ethical decision? If the present national bureaucracies do it, then we are left with what we have now, Cold War and détente in alternation. Possibly, through a combination of unfortunate circumstances, there will be war without warning—after the 130 wars of the "postwar" era a 131st, this time between the two superpowers. The present world situation, in which the bureaucracies of the nation-states are the main protagonists, is laden with the danger of war. It follows that, for peace, a new utopia is essential, and a new protagonist who will dethrone the state bureaucracies from their position of power.

Who can that be? The international working class, as socialists and communists think? No. Every previous attempt has shown that the working class is more national than international. The individual worker's horizons are relatively narrow; those of the nation-state are far wider by comparison. The collective knowledge of a national bureaucracy is so universal alongside that of the average worker that he is defenseless before it. The workers' movement is not intellectually superior to the national bureaucracy; indeed, wherever a political system has arisen that claims legitimacy (usually violently) by reason of representing the working class, a new totalitarian national bureaucracy has taken power, lacking the knowledge and civilized restraints of the old bureaucracy, and hence able with a clear conscience to behave more violently both at home and abroad. Those countries in which the power-wielders claim that the working class is in command are more militarized than the bourgeois countries.

The socialist utopia set out to be more universal than the ideal of the nation-state. In Eastern Europe of the early twentieth century, where the military mentality predominated, and the aristocratic-military bureaucracy of the German Empire, the Austro-Hungarian Monarchy, and the Russian Empire exercised a haughty hegemony over bourgeois society, it was still uncertain which values society would choose—those of military or civil society, command or exchange. In this blinkered world of military parades, what other recourse was there for rebellious bourgeois and petty bourgeois intellectuals and educated young people, hungry for freedom? Where else were they to turn? This was an age when an officer could slap a commoner with impunity, when noblemen predominated in the political bureaucracy (where they could easily appeal to their historic military role of defending the country), and a largely patriotic intellectual bureaucracy set the tone of official culture, dominating the universities and forcing into the marginal situation of dissenters all those thinking people who saw higher values than the values of the fatherland as represented by the military. In such a milieu where should intellectuals of Jewish, worker, or peasant origin turn—intellectuals excluded from the state bureaucracy—except to the only international authority, and the only one that seemed to stand effectively for world peace? That was the international organization of the working class, with its ideology that saw the source of all ills not in national but in social conflicts, and that told the German, Hungarian, and Russian worker that his enemy was not the worker of another nationality, but rather his own rulers. The alternatives were simple enough: either military society or socialist society. Bourgeois society seemed no alternative at all, for the bourgeoisie slavishly subordinated itself to the military-aristocratic bureaucracy.

World War I convinced peace-loving people that the existing society—the alliance of military-aristocratic bureaucracy and large-scale capitalism—led to general war. In what country had the bourgeoisie stood up for the values of peaceful commerce in the face of a military expansionism bent on acquiring markets and sources of raw materials?

The old order, the happy times of peace, had led to the apocalypse of war. Those who wanted peace had proved impotent in the face of the nationalist war psychosis. Jubilant young men had stuck a flower in their hats and gone off to die. Self-sacrificing, noble-minded, hungry for adventure, eager for purification in the ordeal of fire, the young had at first wanted to believe that a new heroic age had come after the banality of bourgeois life. And what was that new heroic life, if not war? A myriad of intellectual influences, philosophies, and artistic currents were concentrated in that great expectant dedication with which the most romantic spirits threw themselves into the slaughter.

Within three years revulsion had set in: in the depths of the trenches, patriotic rhetoric was no longer so inspiring. Once more, international socialism became the order of the day, with its call for an end to the war, for peace—and for world revolution as the way to achieve peace. This battle will be the last one, it promised, then peace will come—just one last effort, one last bloodbath! From the rubble, the international proletariat will build a new Red Europe. Men as astute as Georg Lukacs, appalled at the violence, must have believed something of the sort to leap headfirst into Bolshevism and so into a new, doctrinal violence. For the moment, however, there was no world revolution, and they were the ones under attack. Socialism in one country: for that, it was necessary to steel the workers' fist—the political police, then the Red Army—so it could launch its fraternal tanks to liberate a whole continent from fascism and imperialism, or at a minimum defend that pledge of a brighter future, the world's first socialist state, the harbinger of history's fulfillment: the Soviet Union.

Lenin promised land, peace, and bread. In that way communism attracted the peasants, the soldiers, the workers, and of course the intellectuals, who thought their place was wherever the people's interests lay. And it turned out that the people's interests did not lie with czarism, or with military-aristocratic elitism, or with the cringing Russian bourgeoisie, or with the helpless liberals.

The land was given to the peasants and then taken away again. The collective-farm peasant is as little the master of his own destiny as the peasant of Turgenev and Tolstoy; he is a state serf. And the fewer concessions the state makes to stirrings of initiative among the villagers, the more it keeps them dependent on central direction; the more restrictions it places on independent cultivation and the desire for profit, the more it keeps them in servile, feudal subjection. That is why there is not enough bread even today, sixty-five years after the Revolution. State idolatry cannot grow enough grain. Only enterprising farmers with a stake in what they are doing can grow enough food. Without autonomy there is scarcity and ration coupons.

Peace? Here is the threat of a third world war breathing down our neck: Moscow says Washington is responsible, and Washington says it is Moscow. We might think both responsible, each in a measure difficult to determine. It is a world system, a bipolar system of military blocs, that is to blame, together with that cultural by-product of ideological war, an intelligentsia integrated into the institutional structure of ideological war.

If capitalism is no guarantee against war, neither is communism. Even less reassuring is the world struggle between the two, which a more rigorous analysis would trace to the global rivalry between the two most powerful nation-states of our time and their power elites, waged with methods that can annihilate the civilizations of the northern hemisphere.

IDEOLOGICAL WAR: THE IRRATIONALISM OF OUR TIME

We are past the age of religious wars, perhaps, but we have not yet outlived the age of ideological war, to which many more people may fall victim. In their more exalted moments its acolytes go so far as to suggest that between communism and liberalism no bargain is possible, only victory or death.

How great a role the state budget is to play in redistributing national income—a large one (as in communism), a moderate one (as in social democracy), or a relatively small one (as in liberalism)—is not the sort of question that can be answered by force of arms. The debate between communism and liberalism will not be decided by the death of one human being or a billion. Whether market economy or redistributive economy is more productive, and by how many percentage points, is a matter for empirical study. The most notable economists themselves incline more to value judgments than empirical judgments on this subject.

I turn on the radio: ideological passions, recriminations against the other side. But it isn't really the other side that the Russians and the Americans fear; they are afraid of their own phantoms. Neither wants to attack, but only to guarantee its own security—indeed, to overguarantee it, to the point where its efforts in that direction begin to arouse suspicions. Yet there's nothing to indicate that the balance of terror has increased our security. It's time to look for another guiding strategic doctrine. Our attitude toward nuclear war is like the attitude of a heavy smoker and drinker toward heart attack: he knows there is such a thing but can't imagine it happening to *him*.

Two men can leave a tavern and go out into the alley to decide who's tougher. But this method, alas, isn't available to East and West. Iraq and Iran can pummel each other to their hearts' content because neither one has the atomic bomb. The Soviet Union and the United States cannot because they *do* have atomic bombs—many more than they need. That's really unfair; they ought to have a chance for a scrap, too; otherwise they'll lose their fighting edge and the generals will not be able to conjure up technical miracles of destruction—which would be an infringement of their fundamental human rights.

Let the war ministries square off against each other. Let them convert their destructive intellectual powers into a symbolic public sport with only a theoretical capacity to destroy. Let them devise computerized international war games. Make it an Olympic event, before an impartial jury and a knowledgeable audience. If in this way they could decide periodically which side is able to destroy the other most stunningly, it would not really be necessary to play the game out in real life.

Most of our scientific researchers are paid by the great powers' war ministries, sometimes with the universities acting as go-betweens. Researchers want to research, and if the money for it comes from the military, they will do it for the military. Our technicians are experts in weaponry; our social scientists are experts in ideological war. Bright people go on acting like moral imbeciles. Unless the academic world can acquire economic, moral, and intellectual autonomy, a third world war seems to me inevitable. In an immature world, someone has to assume the mantle of responsible adult authority. Our political and military leaders do not much aspire to this role.

Matters are made no easier by the intellectual agents of our irresponsible power centers, who produce a continuous stream of bellicose and blinkered ideology. When speaking of the other side, they revel in clever critical insights, but regarding their own country or group of countries they are curiously restrained, cautious, tedious, even at times celebratory. They vilify anyone who speaks out against the tribal cult of aggressive ignorance.

Before scholars can acquire independence of their patrons, the intelligentsia—the class that determines our basic cultural values—must learn as a class to act independently and responsibly. It is only fitting that those who think themselves most intelligent should be expected to act most intelligently. Today the universities are our most respected institutions. It is up to them to take on the burden of spiritual authority. Knowing that humanity is one and indivisible, they can relegate the aggressive particularism of individual states to its proper place, in the name of more universal values. The values of the intellectual elite are more international and so more universal than those of the office-holding intelligentsia of the nation-state.

The world champions of provincialism were Hitler and

Stalin. Every society preparing for war is paranoiacally hostile and suspicious toward the outside world. And in the footsteps of the leaders come all the ordinary, small-bore provincials, supremely complacent as they take their short views and cultivate their own little gardens, all helping the big national garden grow under the direction of the head government gardener.

The Iron Curtain is not on our frontiers; it is in our heads. Every time I caution myself against following an idea through to its logical conclusion, I feel the Iron Curtain slam down in my head. I know the hours of inner weakness when the censor's mediocrity looms over me like a house, and here I am, a little bunny in the garden, telling tales about this giant. At such times it's better to be a blockhead than an egghead, and better to be a block of stone than a blockhead.

We have to talk across the Iron Curtain: Eastern and Western Europeans must be permitted to create a European intelligentsia. Peace studies, friendship across the Curtain—these are the over-the-border raids of the intelligentsia against the military status quo and the censor's mediocrity. A bogus peace movement is easily recognized: pompous and empty, it prattles of babies and gets upset at hard thinking. Real peace efforts are inseparable from our everyday work and demand that we make heretical use of the institutional power we have.

What distinguishes us as Europeans is that our thinking patterns are more convoluted, that we handle internal paradoxes more flexibly, that we take pleasure in diversity, that we know how to convert our differences into creative tension, that we can understand and love other cultures and feel sure that we will not lose touch with them. Knowledge and love meet in the concept of understanding. To convert our understanding into the dominant drive of our limited egos—that is the religion of love in contemporary formulation.

The Paradoxical Middle

We who live here in Budapest—right between East and West—we too have something to say. We try to soothe the quarrel, we try to put the bellicose extremes in proper perspective, we play the paradoxical middle; in our own persons we live out the irreconcilable. When the extremes contend, the middle stands to lose the most. By our mere existence, our ideas, and our nimble wits, we try to promote a settlement between communism and capitalism.

To have power, one must want power, and to think, one must want thought; you can't want both. Thinking doesn't require power. The more machinations for power there are, the less thought there is. Reflection and action are not mutually exclusive, but they are dialectical antagonists. There are enough angry people in Central Europe; there is a shortage of thought. Thinking people are needed. We are peacemakers, not revolutionaries. Budapest isn't a bad place to think in. Without a little danger, thinking loses its edge. But too much danger isn't to be recommended.

I don't believe that a new Central European identity will arise on the wings of emotionally charged movements, even mass movements, with the stormy popular tribunes and revolutionary personalities that typically go with them.

Our deepest feelings cannot be mediated by indignation, or anger, or passionate accusations. That is old stuff, yesterday's game, the style of thinking of the anachronistic Left. It is the style of those who appeal melodramatically to others' overheated passions or to the inescapable commands of some historical agenda in order to acquire power for themselves—indeed, an emotionally overblown kind of power.

Nothing would be a bigger mistake for the Eastern European democratic opposition, nothing would hurt our real interests more, than falling captive to the style of thinking, rhetoric, and mythic tendencies of the Jacobin-Leninist tradition. I could only regard as a demagogue anyone who deemed himself a revolutionary today on our political soil.

The reality of Central Europe demands a form of conduct different from that of the communist tradition. In Central Europe, modernity means recognizing the abiding tendencies of our history and applying a sure intuition to extending them; it means recognizing processes that are unfolding and helping them mature, avoiding the clash of ideological and theatrical clichés. Such is the historic enterprise that presents a separate personal challenge to each and every one of us.

Two principles of order face each other, courting Europe on behalf of two different kinds of organization. We may characterize them as diversity or dualism, polycentrism or bipolarity, the many or the two. As the basis for a political program, Europe's cultural diversity has not yet made itself felt.

Europe's political diversity lags far behind its cultural diversity—mostly because of wars, and mostly in our century. One European people or another, organized into a nation-state, has always tried to subject Europe to its own influence, rule, and tutelage. A rival always appeared who tried to prevent it—or rather, tried to appropriate the role for itself. The Latin Papacy and the German Empire contended for it, the English and the Russians, the French and the Germans, not to speak of expanding Islam and more recently the two great federal powers, the Soviet Union and the United States.

The logic of the pre-World War I military alliances arrayed the European nations into two teams: allies and enemies. This division was accomplished in a way that had little more inherent meaning than when children choose up sides in the schoolyard for a soccer game. Our dependence upon the bipolar world model is a primitive and dangerous state of affairs; it doesn't express Europe's historical and social reality, only our subjection to the military status quo and the situation created by World War II, so solemnly invoked in the Soviet press.

Fortunately this dependence is not complete. The European reality is that the French and Germans are refractory allies for the Americans, and the Poles and Hungarians are refractory allies for the Russians. European modernity means that our continent is trying to emancipate itself from the tutelage of the two nuclear world powers, even while extending our ties with both on a basis of equality. We have a European utopia, rooted in our past and present: a wealth of nuance, the art of fine compromise, an apprehension of our environment as art, a wry independence of personality toward the fetishes of state and money, and a sense of man's superiority to his works.

THE SERPENTINE STRATEGY OF EASTERN EUROPEAN LIBERATION

The Eastern European strategy is loose, individual, biological. It grows in the direction of the possible; it feels its way along the path of least resistance. It is cautious about formulating things too explicitly, it doesn't say everything straight out, it avoids open, institutional, sharply defined forms. It moves relentlessly, mysteriously, tortuously; it can wait a long time, then suddenly spring.

The bearer of the Eastern European strategy is the individual who enters and leaves institutional groupings only conditionally, who is suspicious of everything organized, yet knows that organization is unavoidable. POWER does not exist; everywhere there are people, prone to act in unaccountable ways, sometimes helpful, sometimes harmful.

Our social organization is not Western European, nor is our strategy of self-defense. Our society is not quite grown up, not completely rational; it is a little too childish and a little too old to be rational in the Western European way. We are in cahoots not only with our friends but also with others—strangers—and of course even with those whom we consider, for the sake of the game, our enemies.

Our defeats are milestones on the road to Eastern European liberation. Defeat is part of the game; we will not be cast down by it for long, we will get up and go on, and if we don't, then our children will. The Eastern European strategy is tenacious; catastrophes are its schoolbooks. There is no total defeat; each defeat shows how the road is winding, shows which way to go if you can't continue in the same direction. On a winding road there is a greater likelihood of accidents.

It is almost as if this series of experiments were one continuing experiment, conducted by the same experimenter. Hungarians, Czechs, Poles—after three tries and three mistakes (in which we each sketched our portrait clearly) we looked around at one another with considerable familiarity. Something painful and ridiculously similar happened to all three of us. It appears that we are partners in destiny. Are we insulted and humiliated? That would be an exaggeration—not quite East Central European; it has a Russian ring.

The trials that all three of us have made are our common past. The post-World War II period has renewed our alliance: historically, we are kin. We have said before that "we Czechs are not Hungarians," "we Poles are not Czechs," "we Hungarians are not Poles." There wasn't much point in that. We are Hungarians and Poles and Czechs and—the list could go on. The strivings of every people of our area for freedom are ours.

Our area is the area of the Soviet empire. We would like to democratize our relationship with the Russians, transforming it into an international community of partners. Our interests demand that Moscow not be the center of a colossal empire, because if it is, we are not sovereign. We have an interest in the reorganization of the empire into equal, fraternal republics. We have a stake in seeing it happen without bloodshed.

Centralized political authority is one pole; decentralized spiritual authority is the other. At one pole is executive power; at the other, inquiry. Here in Eastern Europe the scholars have succeeded at some things, the executives at others. Perhaps our imaginations were too feeble, if our reality is so banal.

It would be well if political and intellectual authority could deal with each other on a higher plane and with more mutual respect. Intellectual authority should not try to be political authority, and political authority should not want to be intellectual authority. By respecting each other's independence, they could learn from each other.

The summits of political power are occupied by designated figures. They can be dismissed and replaced even when shielded from the risks of democratic competition. In that case, their fall comes about not at elections but in the world of secret conferences. But intellectual authority has no summit. It is like a forest: there are smaller and larger trees, but each is only one tree. The forest is as dense as our common spiritual condition. Those who stand in the tower —do they hear the rustling of the forest? Do they feel the democracy of the oaks?

In every village and every workshop there are people whom others listen to. Everywhere there are clusters of old people and of audacious youth. A network of spiritual authority exists. We know of one another. We know one another. We know what we think of one another. We know what everyone thinks of everyone else. We have no very great secrets from one another. We could not really surprise one another. Our shamefaced common consciousness is beginning to raise its head. If we really knew who we were. we could turn the tanks into grazing lambs.

Spiritual authority expresses our mute common knowledge. The baker bakes bread in our stead, the fencer fences in our stead, the writer writes in our stead. It would be well if we all knew how to bake, to fence, to write.

There is no need to give the fabric of spiritual authority a name, nor does it need to be installed in some public building. Spiritual authority is solidarity. The chairman of Solidarity was an electrician with six children, a man just as fallible, wily, and stubborn as we are. It was good to have Solidarity rather than just solidarity. What remains is solidarity with a small letter, something rather like the intimacy of travelers on a slow train. It's a good thing if the passengers start talking with one another as if they were old friends.

No thinking person should want to drive others from positions of political power in order to occupy them himself. I would not want to be a minister in any government whatever. I feel much better at my writing table than I would at any minister's desk, where I would have to puzzle over texts of official documents. I prefer to decide about words rather than people. Anyway, I suspect that ministers are more afraid of losing their portfolios to their deputies than to independent thinkers.

If the moral opposition tries to act like a political opposition, it may soon find that millions are standing behind it and asking, "Where do we go from here?" My worst nightmare is to have to tell millions of people what to do next. The opposition thinker is not a member of any shadow cabinet. He doesn't much care who the ministers are today or who the next ones will be. I would not want the government in power to feel threatened. If it is frightened, it is capable of casting aside all constitutional moderation and exchanging the methods of a conservative authoritarianism for those of totalitarian rule.

I ask the authorities not to feel themselves threatened by the independent intelligentsia. I ask the intelligentsia not to alarm the authorities. Grown people should not threaten; they should deal like sensible, well-brought-up Europeans. Bluster, arrogance, and conceit are never civilized behavior. It would be well for my friends—independent intellectuals, oppositionists, people on the fringes, dissidents, critics of the system, protesters, violators of the censorship, people who have been shown the door or banned—if the authorities themselves were to want some of the same things that we want. It doesn't say much for the reputation of our wares if we are unable to sell any of our ideas at all to those in power.

In fact, those who hold the leading positions are not the worst consumers of ideas. In the last analysis they are intellectuals, too: they enjoy reading interesting material— material not written under their control. They hope to find things in it that they too may be able to use sometime without losing their jobs.

In the market where ideas are exchanged, we are at their disposal, too (and also at the disposal of strike organizers, of course). We have to be clear about who is playing what game. If our role is clear, we can tolerate one another more easily. If our self-definition lacks precision, there can be no relative consensus. We can only give the advice we believe in, even if it is unwelcome advice. Everything goes to serve the beauty of the social game.

I am not calling for militant mass pressure against the politicians. It's not becoming for mature men to fear that they will be beaten; how much better if we can instill their superegos with our values. There's no reason why the executive intelligentsia should think exactly the same as the creative intellectuals, but is there any reason why they have to think the exact opposite?

We live in a crabbed society, and what I am most interested in is how we can make it less crabbed. I miss having a world view adequate to our situation and affording some evidence of real self-knowledge. I take reality for a game and would like to understand the various strategies. I would like to know along what lines we could get in touch more productively.

People with independent perceptions should put their views at the disposal of every actor in our system. We ought to think things through from the standpoint of the system as a whole. Our brand of two-fisted intellectual is ambivalent: he likes a good game, but he likes his sanguinary theater, too. We have to redeem the general interests of the intellectual class from a narrow minority of that class—the political bureaucracy. It rests with the opposition to take up the constructive task of reflecting, free of censorship, on the question of a democratic reform of state socialism (or state capitalism). And it rests with them to reflect, without self-deception, on the strategic dilemmas that confront the intellectual class.

One feasible undertaking for the opposition would be to formulate, freely and critically, the ideology of a reform program that could be carried through from the top down. There must be some long-range strategic conjunction of interests between the powers that be and the moral and intellectual authority that would monitor them. Bad communication leads to murder. In this many-sided game of ours, I see the refinement of the rules of the game as our ethical obligation.

The results of our thinking are determined by our interests. Our interests, here in Budapest, can be formulated as follows: what can still be done, when it's almost impossible to do anything? In Poland, our friends who tried in good faith to do something are in jail. On the government side, the Hungarian regime is the one that has given the most successful answer to this question. It has assembled the most smoothly functioning communist system—one not threatened by major dangers either internal or external. Here it's possible to think in the sharpest terms about the reformability of communism.

The great psychic test of the radical political opposition is this: can it identify with the viewpoints of the other players in our system? Critical principles don't make it any easier to analyze and understand what we have now. Fortunately, the Hungarian opposition is more cultural and theoretical in character, and its own preferences don't greatly interfere with its labor of understanding.

Nowhere else are the chances any better. In the East, the

official analysts think in precensored terms and write in apologetic ones. Conservative Western writers, in opposing their own leftists and hoping for a Soviet collapse, offer a moralizing liberal critique of the Soviet system. Western left-wing critics ruminate over the degeneration of existing forms of socialism, in the name of whichever abstract model of socialism they want. Neither of these is a promising position.

Beneath the surface, the independent intelligentsia carries out a fundamental labor. By transforming society's image of itself, it transforms conditions. The ideology of democratic liberation is a nonviolent one; it strives to develop autonomous tempers that are steadfast and know how to wait. The democratic movement would still be in a morally superior position, even if the authorities resorted to a flurry of repressive measures.

The ideology of the democratic opposition shares with religion a belief that the dignity of the individual personality (in both oneself and the other person) is a fundamental value not requiring any further demonstration. The autonomy and solidarity of human beings are the two basic and mutually complementary values to which the democratic movement relates other values. To that extent, it stands close to the Judaeo-Christian ethic. Autonomy and solidarity are the root values of every democratic ideology. No philosophy has yet succeeded in calling these two complementary values into question for long. Those who betray these values, on the other hand, are usually reduced to hypocrisy.

The culture of autonomy protests against making any

human institution superior to the dignity of individual human beings. Whenever the state, or some power bloc, or the world market comes to be regarded as an absolute value, this opposition will appear, invoking the European tradition in order to demonstrate that this allegedly supreme value is really far from universal, and is in fact only the special interest of a certain group of people. It is precisely this critique of ideology that offers the Eastern European democratic opposition a way to contribute to the culture of self-determination for individuals, for groups, for the nation, and for the continent as a whole.

The Framework Stays, the Rest Is Reformable

Between them, internal weaknesses and occupations from without have created here a syndrome of limited independence: we are not fully grown up as either a nation or a society. Among us the relations of civil society, based on equality, are less common, and relations of subordination are more widespread. We are by no means Western Europeans, but we don't belong to the East either, for the logic of empire doesn't attract us.

Our grotesque little hegemonies go together with our subjection. We were petty lords, never really colonizers, neither servants nor masters. Our tutelage to a great power determines not only our alliance status but our social arrangements as well. The cardinal proof of our loyalty to the alliance is the fact that we maintain a Soviet-type political structure, with an authoritarian one-party system.

That system can come in more totalitarian or more paternalistic versions, with stricter or more permissive styles; it can be more open or more closed. It can repress divergent opinions at once, but it can also tolerate them up to a point. Its subtypes may vary, but the vital working principles of the general type cannot be called into question for long without provoking direct or indirect punitive action from the imperial center. The Soviet army not only ensures that the member states will remain true to their alliance system; it also guarantees that no strong independent organization will curtail the hegemonic rule of state parties more or less loyal to Moscow.

The three spontaneously emerging desires of the peoples of East Central Europe—for neutrality, a multiparty system, and self-government within the structure of the empire—are incompatible. It turns out, nevertheless, that the three demands go together. Each one implies the next. One level of self-determination for a society cannot be walled off sharply from another. Military retaliation has followed each time one of the peripheral countries tried to free itself from any essential structural feature of the Soviet model. Loyalty to the Soviet Union and to the local party is the sine qua non of the system.

It would be self-delusion to think that we can fool Moscow. The Soviet ruling elite isn't soft-hearted, it never loses sight of its own interests, and it doesn't shrink in the face of international outcries once it has made up its mind to defend its perceived vital interests vigorously; nor can it be persuaded that its interests would be served if the peripheral countries regained their independence. Democracy and independence, here and now, are not possible for us; the basic framework of political and economic power cannot be reformed to the point where new decision-making centers, independent of the imperial power center and incapable of being reabsorbed into it, might arise. Genuine reform would occur only if the independence of new centers of legitimate decision-making power were guaranteed by some sort of legal and constitutional tribunal.

We have constantly tried to move in the direction of these dreams of ours, step by modest step, and yet without ever really getting close to them. The framework remains; the rest, however, can be worked on. By comparison with the institutional system of power, the spirit and style in which power is exercised is more flexible and can be changed. It is impossible to overestimate the importance of the good will of the officials, their sensitivity and good sense, the fairness of some individuals. Where the official stratum is humane, even authoritarianism is bearable. Those who run the state bear a larger personal responsibility, and it is possible to awaken that sense of responsibility by bringing them under the scrutiny of the public. Blaming the basic framework for everything only relieves them of all responsibility.

For historical materialism there are no good capitalists and bad capitalists; all capitalists are exploiters. The spirit of textbook Marxism (as opposed to a more realistic, critical socialism) tends to look at Party and government functionaries in the same insensitive way. The democratic opposition ought to free itself of this kind of abstract, unhistorical outlook and reintroduce into its thinking the ethos of personal moral responsibility. What sort of people wield power over us is very important, and even if we don't like the framework of power that weighs upon us, it is important that we applaud intelligent and honest leaders and show our personal moral disapproval of those who choose, from all the decisions open to them within the given institutional structure, the stupidest and most harmful ones. We should show understanding when our leaders put aside goals that stand no chance of being attained and concentrate on those that have some prospect (by no means certain) of achievement. The main objective of the democratic movement should be to spread the idea that the execution of a national strategy requires a division of labor, and that people in different positions who respect one another can permit themselves, in varying degrees, to be open and to take risks in order to discharge well the obligations laid upon them.

The Hungarian political leadership, it seems to me, has no illusions about Moscow; they know with whom they have to deal. For that reason, the leadership is able to strike a relative balance between the desires of Hungarian society and those of the Russian elite. To the extent that they are national politicians and play a mediating role—to the extent that they can simultaneously weigh local and imperial interests in making their decisions—the East Central European leaders can afford to show some slight (though not conspicuous) preference for local interests.

The Soviet empire is still vigorous, it would seem, in spite of its internal difficulties; it is far from doomed to collapse under the impact of internal or external conflicts. There is no reason, then, for us to place our hopes in radical structural changes. The best we can hope to achieve is an enlightened, paternalistic authoritarianism, accompanied by a measured willingness to undertake gradual liberal reforms. For us, the least of all evils is the liberal-conservative version of communism, of the sort we see around us in Hungary. If we cannot hope without deluding ourselves, what kind of hope can we have? For us, is there any alternative to the resigned careerism of those in government?

It is also possible to conclude that we were born in an irredeemably ill-starred corner of the earth and that there is only one way to overcome this misfortune—by leaving it for some happier soil. The other way is to attempt the near-impossible: even if our nation and our institutions have no autonomy, to try to work out our own.

I have chosen the latter. I have decided not to take leave of this country permanently. If I can, I will travel for a year or two, familiarizing myself with other cultures so as to view our conditions from a distance. I will cross the Iron Curtain, leaving most of myself here while a part of me sees the West. I am a Central European; here my attitudes are Western European, there they are Eastern European.

Some mad East Central European folly keeps me here; possibly the intoxication of inner freedom compensates for the painful absence of external liberty. At other times I think that this is the only place where there is really something to think about, since even geographically this is the center of Europe.

If Budapest, Bratislava, Prague, Cracow, Warsaw, and Berlin belong to Europe, then why not Leningrad, why not Moscow—indeed, why stop before Vladivostok? It is all part of Eurasia, there is no state frontier between. It is possible to think on a Eurasian scale, too. This is a more fitting perspective for the next millennium than that of little Western Europe, from where the life I live here seems an alien mythology. I would like to think of myself as some utopian son of Europe, able to touch the Pacific at San Francisco with one outstretched arm and at Vladivostok with the other, and keeping the peace everywhere within my embrace.

I have the Russians to thank for my life; of all the literatures of the world, that of Russia has affected me the most. Yet I see the role of the Russians in Europe as the biggest question mark for the cause of world peace. It would be foolish for me to pretend that we don't think about them. I know of no way for Eastern Europe to free itself from Russian military occupation except for us to occupy them with our ideas. Think about it: in a free exchange of ideas, who would colonize whom?

"You are the Swiss bankers of Eastern Europe," a French journalist exclaimed to me one day in the fall of 1980 in Warsaw, when I told him that we were sympathetic spectators of the Polish drama, but that with our reflexes we couldn't imagine any more livable brand of communism for the present than our conservative-liberal authoritarianism, tempered by strivings for greater efficiency. We Hungarians never created our own KOR* or Solidarity, because we

---

* Acronym for the Workers' Defense Committee (Komitet Obrony Robotników), a group of some thirty Polish intellectuals formed in September 1976 to mobilize public opinion in defense of workers involved in the protests of June 1976. In time KOR developed into an openly antitotalitarian opposition movement of wide scope. [Publisher's note.]

didn't really believe that communist power could be reconciled with democratic institutions born of society's aspirations for self-determination. We saw what our Polish friends were doing; we wanted them to succeed, but doubted that they could.

"Be careful," I said to Adam, "the third time around it has to work." It didn't. Adam is awaiting trial perhaps. "It's incredible," he said: incredible that he was able to give a lecture at the Warsaw Polytechnic University on 1956 in Poland and Hungary. The lecture was first-rate: he didn't stammer at all; he was sharp, dialectical, and got to the heart of the matter. Then they said he fell madly in love with a great actress. Then they said he was arrested and beaten half to death. Then they said he was all right. What does it all tell us, Adam? You are thirty-five million, but you couldn't pull it off; now what?

What would you say if I told you: "Now let the Russians do it"? Since we are yoked together this way anyhow, let's try to win them over to our game. They allow us only a little more freedom than they allow themselves. Obviously, if we want much more freedom for ourselves, we have to want more freedom for them as well. It's our most basic interest to persuade them to reform, because that's in their interest as much as our own.

A glimmer of light briefly in one country, then in another—then darkness again. The national road to Eastern European liberation has not carried us very far; bloc-wide exchanges of ideas and reform experiments have never been tried. For that, partners are needed. We look at them nervously, to be sure, but if they are to be our partners in reform, we have to look them squarely in the eye.

The strategy of peace strives to win over the other person, not overwhelm him. It seeks not to fight but to reach agreement, to strike a bargain in a calm spirit of mutual affinity. Fighting and negotiating are both forms of self-assertion; if fighting doesn't work, then we negotiate. But is fighting better than negotiating? Or is it only a necessary evil, done for lack of anything better? In our culture, people who negotiate are feeling less and less shame toward those who fight.

Today we need a real strategy, something that history will later be able to read from our conduct today. I see it more in the conduct of individuals than in that of groups—individual reactions, which are not really analytical and logical, and for which politics is not the most natural language. Our people fought against and lived with Turks, Germans, and Russians—more than that, they conquered them, conquered them from below even while the Hungarians themselves lay conquered and supine. They had, as it were, a dual consciousness: that of the warrior who scorns all negotiation, and that of the negotiator who shies away from the warrior and tries to get by on his wits. In this area the language of politics is banal and impoverished; our effectiveness is greater, the more distant we remain from politics.

Our mode of expression is marked by a sentimental and humorous worldly wisdom, by a knowing archness, by jokes, by sly exchanges of winks: "I know what I know and you know what you know." Looking at them from a distance, I find considerable resemblance between my progovernment and opposition friends; Budapest is written all over all of them. However long a face they may pull, their hidden humor has the savor of Budapest's cynicism in it. What is it that those who stay here, can't bear to give up and those who leave remember with longing? What is it that we really find good in our life here, what is it in the last analysis that we like in ourselves? Perhaps it is this vitality of ours, our slyness, our roguishness, our guile.

There are traces in us of conqueror and conquered. Finno-Ugrians, Bulgars, Khazars, Slavs, Pechenegs, Cumans, Tartars, Romanians, Turks, Germans, Jews, Serbs, Slovaks, Russians, Greeks, gypsies—what *is* a Hungarian, anyway? A Danubian mixture, with the common savoir vivre of intermingled people; resourceful, capable of rising from defeat and putting bad luck to good use; the mixed consciousness of nobles and serfs, of the arrogant and the meek. Here, between haughty lords and humble servants, a self-respecting citizen is maturing in the larva of the state-socialist man.

This self-respecting mean is still inchoate. We lack a clear self-portrait which would display to us the balancing act with which we handle our wretched paradoxes. If we cannot command destiny, we slyly try to get round it. Our people are engaging in politics today with means that are not those of politics, as they putter in the garden or expound over their wine, or as a speaker makes his audience chuckle by very nearly saying what he is thinking and making a joke about what he doesn't say. This Central European strategy is a delicate thing. You will find it in our government officials, even those who are sick of government; the spirit of the same literature is at work in them, too.

We have to do without democratic political institutions, and so we do without them. Whether or not we give a name to our friendly get-togethers is unimportant. If they have no name, they can't be banned. We have no Solidarity, but we can still have solidarity, which can't be suspended. Friendship cannot be outlawed. Our organizations are networks of sympathy; we have no headquarters and no leaders, so it is harder to touch us. We are crafty, cautious game; we don't make it any easier for the hunter to bag us.

THE DEMAND FOR SELF-GOVERNMENT IN EASTERN EUROPE

The idea of delegated authority has become problematical. There is less reason all the time why grown, educated, intelligent people should transfer their powers of decision to distant, unknown, and scarcely accountable individuals, as if selecting guardians to make their decisions for them. It would seem more natural if authority and labor, administration and everyday life were to be separated as little as possible.

Solidarity was an authentic socialist working-class movement; it was a sign that throughout state-socialist society the demand has awakened for the producers to manage and govern themselves. It is natural that a new, better-educated working class requires less direction from above than the old, unskilled work force did. It is natural that trained specialists are generally quite as intelligent as their superiors. The difference in knowledge between leaders and led grows smaller all the time. Indeed, the intellectuals who staff our institutions are better educated than those at the top.

Communism has sanctioned a system in which the more stupid lead the more intelligent, because it has made political reliability a more important job requirement than ability. Managers in Eastern Europe are overwhelmingly Party members because if they were not, they would not be managers. This is the unwritten law of countries where the antifeudal revolution was never really carried through, where the equality of citizens before the law has never really been achieved.

To insist on the leading role of the Party is to admit that democracy does not and should not exist. It's like saying that Party members have a feudal right to the overwhelming majority of leadership posts; or, to put it the other way around, that non-Party people are excluded from leading positions. Only one out of every ten adults is a Party member, yet three-quarters of our leaders are Party members. A young person who doesn't join the Party forfeits all hope of a career. In communist countries non-Party people are second-class citizens. They may achieve success and a good income, but never power; they remain excluded from the important decisions. In communist countries power is the greatest value, and power belongs to Party people alone. To be a convinced communist today means to be convinced that you and your associates have a natural right to the leadership roles, together with the favors and privileges that go with them.

Since this state of affairs constantly offends the sense of justice of the nine-tenths who are outside the Party, and since the rule of the one-tenth over the nine-tenths can be maintained only by means of an elaborate police state, communist power by its very structure creates the potential for a democratic revolution. In Eastern Europe, reform means gradually doing away with the neofeudal privileges of Party members. Need we ask how enthusiastically the Party members officially assigned to that task will leap to their work? How badly does the Party want to see any considerable number of key posts slip from its grasp? I know Party members who sympathize with democracy, but only in their weaker moments, rather like Moslems with their wine.

For the most part, Eastern European social movements—especially workers' movements—have not demanded multiparty, parliamentary, representative democracy, but rather workplace self-management and direct democracy. That is quite understandable and by no means simply a reflection of "geopolitical necessity."

Speaking of geopolitical givens, we frequently observe that the Soviet leadership forbids multiparty systems in Eastern Europe, calling them counterrevolutionary. If the majority of a population tries to create democracy, that also, in communist parlance, is counterrevolution. Historically, this aversion is understandable, for constitutional, parliamentary government has not found favor within the walls of the Kremlin since the day they were built.

We have often heard the Soviet press call attempts at worker self-management counterrevolutionary, too. If the Party leaders of a fraternal socialist country were to agree to a real sharing of power with the real working class, that would be revisionist opportunism on their part, and on the workers' part it would be antisocialist counterrevolution. Those intellectuals who spread the idea of self-management are, again, agents of imperialism. We have seen that every independent structure—direct, self-managing democracy as well as indirect, parliamentary democracy—is incompatible with the framework of Yalta, which is essentially military in character.

We might, indeed should, mention socialist democracy, too, only we shouldn't understand it to mean anything that really exists. Theoretically, one might suppose that the words implied a multiparty system of government, with self-management in the workplace and in local communities. In theory, there would be nothing objectionable in that. In practice, however, it is inadmissible. In practice, socialist democracy is forbidden. If it does appear, the tanks roll and the prisons fill.

Of course "greater democratism" is desirable. It looks better when the decisions of the Party leadership are voted unanimously by organizations whose leaders are nominated from above but then elected from below. But in the countries of the Soviet bloc, socialist democracy means that the people who sit on the platform under Lenin's portrait tell us what's going to happen, while the people in the audience applaud the speakers—at length, rhythmically, sometimes rising to their feet. We say that one of these countries is liberal if it is not necessary to rise and if it is possible to stop applauding a little sooner.

It is understandable if factory workers take as much interest—or more—in who makes the decisions in the factory as they do in who makes the decisions in the government. They know the decision makers in the factory but not, presumably, the ones in the government. The government is far away, the factory management is close at hand. A worker stands a much better chance of being elected to the works council than he does of becoming a parliamentary deputy.

In Eastern Europe today, self-management is society's prime demand wherever one can express such demands openly. It is a matter of common observation that the workers don't want to exchange their government-appointed managers for capitalist owner-managers. They want chiefs they themselves elect, ones whom they can monitor and who can be replaced—chiefs who will not lord it over the collective but will coordinate its ideas with those of the various groups of specialists, translating the resulting rough consensus into the language of managerial decisions.

Workplace and local community self-government, based on personal contact, exercised daily, and always subject to correction, have a greater attraction in our part of the world than multiparty representative democracy because, if they have the choice, people are not content with voting once every four years just to choose their deputy or the head of the national government. That somehow seems very little when people hope that, by taking a part in the affairs of the community, they can gain a voice in their own destiny.

When there is parliamentary democracy but no self-administration, the political class alone occupies the stage. The people's role is limited to choosing, from among various candidates, those who will shine upon this stage. The visible part of the stage is the screen. The politician talks, the viewer listens. Until the next election, the viewer has only the same rights as the citizen of Eastern Europe: he can turn off the television. The interesting thing about direct democracy is that the audience takes an active part, too.

The message is clear in the resolutions drawn up by the workers' councils during the Hungarian revolution of 1956: multiparty parliamentary democracy is essential; self-governance in every concrete community is essential. Democracy is essential at every level. It occurred to no one to expatiate on how this would be a good thing at some levels but a bad thing at other levels. It was the dramaturgical function of 1956 to state the essential, without beating around the bush. Democracy is needed in factory management, in the government, and in relations with other governments. We need it in self-defense, so that others will not be able to humiliate, ruin, occupy, and terrorize us.

The notion of self-governing factories and cities, not subject to Party authority, is at least as attractive as that of a division of the political class into two or more party leaderships which would then compete for ministerial posts, appealing for votes by means of advertising, media publicity, and sonorous speeches.

We can defend ourselves against the political class's monopoly if we ourselves manage our real business as far as possible—we whose lives are directly affected, we who know something about it because we live in the midst of it. We may sometimes mistake our interests, but less often perhaps than those who know better than we do where our interests lie and who use informers to remind us that we had better believe they know better.

People in Eastern Europe are thoroughly fed up with those mentors who know better than they do what they need. If they once get the power of self-determination in their hands, they will not readily let go of it again. They won't be willing to confide it to new spellbinders. They are suspicious of political forums, where they have always been deceived. Eastern Europeans identify politics with fraud, with something that's no business of theirs. They have grown unaccustomed to the idea that even in parliament the truth can be spoken. But now they can imagine, in their bolder dreams, that one could speak the truth on the shop floor or in the office conference room.

I can't convince the national authorities of anything, but I can convince my friends and colleagues of a thing or two. I was last in the parliament to look around when I was eight years old, but I used to go to the office every day and I met with my friends every day. Clearly, the democracy that exists where I am means more to me than the democracy that exists someplace where I am not.

Self-management means that representative democracy spreads from the political sphere to the economic and cultural spheres as well. It means that democracy is the prevailing principle of legitimacy in the factory, in the research institute, in every institution—not Party rule or corporate rule.

I understand perfectly that the Polish workers' movement which rallied around Solidarity was not much liked by either the Party power centers or corporate boards of directors. At most, Western politicians expressed sympathy for it in order to annoy the Soviet politburo, if and when they wanted to annoy it. And if they didn't want to, they made no secret of the fact that they didn't greatly care for a movement that radically undermined the power monopoly of every political class.

In the capitalist democracies politics is liberal and democratic, while the economy is hierarchically organized and directed from the top down, responding to the decisions of the owners. Trade unions limit the power of management more by defending the rights and income of the workers than by influencing economic and technical decisions or the organization and quality of life of the enterprise. It is certainly no accident that self-management has become a fundamental demand in precisely those places where capitalist rule has ceased to be legitimate. In Eastern Europe, the demand for democracy makes itself felt in every social organization, in economic and cultural as well as political institutions.

One might well suppose that democracy would become the universal principle of legitimacy in those societies that we could call postcommunist and at the same time postcapitalist. Today there are no such societies anywhere. The Hungarians, the Czechs, and the Poles made an attempt to create such a society for themselves. That the attempt was put down by armed force is no proof that it was impossible in principle; much less is it evidence against the attractive force of the ideal.

In Yugoslavia, economic democracy is limited by the absence of political democracy. In general, no one whom the Party opposes can become the head of one of the organs of self-management; only Party members are eligible—people who by joining the Party have accepted the principle that only Party members can govern. And if Party members head the organs of self-management, then obviously they are bound by party discipline to obey the higher Party authorities. A structural conflict exists between the Party leadership and self-management.

The Hungarian national and factory committees of 1945, when the old state order collapsed, and the revolutionary and workers' councils of 1956, when the new state order likewise collapsed—two systems directed from above by command methods—proclaimed instantly and forcefully the people's lack of confidence in leaders outside their control, whom they had put up with only from necessity. They also proclaimed their confidence in themselves—being no stupider than the leaders—and in their ability to provide their own leadership.

Passing over the Czechoslovak experiment for the moment, it is clear that in Poland Solidarity was a great deal more than a trade union. It was a movement for social self-defense just as KOR was a committee for social self-defense, only instead of thirty members it had ten million. There's nothing surprising in the fact that no organizational model exists for the internal self-management of a movement ten million strong, including virtually all of society. Small wonder if there was no ready-made theory and methodology waiting for it, or that what worked for thirty people who could all fit into the same room didn't work for ten million, for whom communicating with one another was a problem in itself.

Now that they have driven it underground, it may not be a mark of insufficient solidarity to ask ourselves: in the context of a statist society, in the world of Yalta, is it possible to imagine an independent self-defense organization on a nationwide scale (actually mirroring the articulation of the state administration itself) that is capable of self-management? If it is not centralized there is no coordination, and if it *is* centralized there is no self-management.

Whatever we think about the viability of Solidarity, as it was, in the Soviet empire, and whether or not we think it was well conceived (indeed, it wasn't conceived at all, it just happened, like a sudden storm), Solidarity's unexpected vigor and popularity confirms the hypothesis that in the state-socialist societies democracy in the broadest sense is now on the historical agenda. Democracy is on our minds: it is what we crave the most because it is what we lack the most, in every sphere of activity, in our economy and culture as much as in politics—and especially in those areas where we meet face to face and can look in the eye the people who make the decisions in our name and order us to carry them out.

Since these people constantly say that they decide in our best interests, let them at last decide in our best interests! Communist-style socialism promises more democracy than liberal capitalism, but it delivers less. It's not surprising if from time to time society has enough of this monumental fraud and takes the state at its word. We are stockholders in a corporation whose directors, whenever the stockholders try to call them to account, respond by calling out their tanks.

The Polish democratic movement has demonstrated that it is impossible to want freedom a little. If a little freedom exists, more is wanted, then more and still more, until a new constitutional and institutional system, approved by all, comes into being. Then and only then will a new, stable political equilibrium appear, one that cannot be called into question in the light of democratic principles.

The independent social movement rejected central direction of the economy and state monopoly of the media of communication. On the most important issues involving organizational structure, it rejected the absolute sovereignty of the Party state. It demanded the right to make its own decisions, as a community eager to govern itself.

Until an institutional system of pluralist democracy is constructed, there will be no stable authority. Either authority relies on terrorizing society, or else it accepts popular electoral decisions. Soviet-type states cannot consent to elections that could replace the legitimacy of Soviet-type rule with a radically different kind of legitimacy—that of the sovereignty of popular electoral expression, which makes the will of the majority law whether the Party state likes it or not. The Party state cannot submit to the will of the majority because, if it did, it would cease to be a Party state. At critical junctures, however, the majority demands that the Party state submit to it. At critical moments the majority expects voting to be more than a hollow farce.

Self-management is really the question of questions; it deserves a referendum. The moderates, the believers in compromise, hoped for some kind of sensible accommodation, but a situation has arisen where this is now an either/or question. Should property belong to the state or to society? Who should name the leaders—superior authority, or a body elected by the working people? Should sovereignty come from above or from below?

If economic decisions are not to be legitimized by capitalist ownership of property, then either the government must legitimize them or else the associated producers collectively. If it is the latter, then there arises the key question for self-management: who decides in the name of the associated producers? An elected body or person? Or is it possible to create a flexible legal and financial system, with social property at the disposal of individuals, which could serve as an economic formula for self-management?

Our liberal reformers like to obscure this question, but reform would be limited indeed if it were legitimized from the top down. The state is not going to take state property and make it social property. If the right of decision remains at the top, then the higher authorities will permit the lower economic organs only as much autonomy as suits them, the higher authorities. They will share their redistributive economic power in such a way that in all essential strategic matters there will still be no disputing it. If they do give autonomy, they will try to limit and obstruct it in every way and to take it back again on essential points. The apex of the pyramid is its magnetic center. The machinery of power has its own internal structural integrity. Under a leadership appointed from above on the basis of loyalty, there can be no competitive independence. The Polish state decided on December 13, 1981: state property remains! There will be no social property or self-management! Those who have the weapons make the decisions.

The Polish power elite, with the Soviet power elite behind it, demonstrated that it was no paper tiger. In Eastern Europe it is impossible to democratize society by trying to overthrow the local elite. Nor was that the way it was done in southern Europe: in Spain, Portugal, and Greece the process of democratization was not a revolutionary one. The political elites were not overthrown; a more broadly based middle class and technocracy simply absorbed them. A middle-class intelligentsia on the road to embourgeoisement swallowed up the political bureaucracy of dictatorship.

The power elites in these three countries were able to evolve from premodern, hierarchically organized elites into modern, pluralistic ones. Human beings were not swept away or thrown into prison; no one was, in communist parlance, "liquidated"; whole classes and social groups were not tossed into "the dustbin of history." Nothing happened except that the iceberg of power was melted from within.

The old recipe called for the overthrow of the machinery of power by means of a mass movement. The new recipe calls for a transformation of the political structure by means of a slowly ripening social transformation. Political changes must be preceded by social changes. Mass movements will not modify or weaken the power structure of either military bloc in any significant way. It seems to me that the Hungarian way is more the way of social change, while the Polish way was more the way of political change. These two ways are not mutually exclusive, but the difference of emphasis is not negligible.

Our Polish friends were taken within hours to their camps. What can they possibly mean by a prison camp in peacetime? As soon as an atrocity becomes news it is already less of an atrocity, more just a piece of news.

Folly is to be expected, good sense is improbable; tank

treads have no sense. Defeat can be survived, but the curfew is still visible in the faces of passers-by. Fear seeps in through the keyhole, the silent telephone listens; clean white prison shirts lie in the bureau drawer. Loyalty oaths: first give yourself up, then others. Shrinking circles of friends, fenced in without any fault on our part. Here tragedy, there imperial reason. Sound the trumpet, fools! The country is yours, power is yours.

The lesser evil? All these damned lesser evils put together! The angry little old man gestured and said, "Shit!" If in spite of everything people don't crave freedom, then they're not much different from what they ingest and excrete.

Why should they let them out? Violence must be prolonged until there is no resistance left. Everyone who had reason to fear before is coming forward and taking his revenge. You may not break, but will you wear out after a while? Monuments of 1956, monuments of 1968, monuments of 1981, all together in one friendly company. Defeat always begins when we realize, bitterly and logically, that they have superior force and we are helpless. If I were not firmly convinced that freedom waits at the end of the road, I would give up the game. One can retreat, seek another way, fall silent, go underground—but not give up.

The minority is analyzing its actions behind bars. "How many times has your house been searched?" I asked Adam. "Forty-five," he replied cheerfully. No wonder there's so much interest in his writings. Limited democratic institutions, a social contract, independent political structures—at present, it appears, these things will not work within the framework of Yalta. Little circles of friends, of independent people, go on. We are groping for a firm basis, a level beneath which it would be impossible to sink.

Solidarity will rise again. The demand for self-government will rise again. These ideas cannot be buried. The teachings of Christ recommended nonviolence to the Catholic Poles. It is not the violent ones who are brave, but rather the people on whom violence has no hold. The peaceful power of the plain-spoken truth is hard to finish off. It was the government, not Solidarity, that resorted to weapons. Solidarity didn't hit back, and it did well not to do so. It is waiting; it is not storming the public squares, but it is at home in every dwelling.

We languish in the depths of defeat. Is it possible that the monolith can never be moved off of us? The only ones who never suffer defeat are those who consent to everything. Failure is not a fault but a fulfillment, the last act of a bold experiment. I believe not in victory but in the stubbornness of a few. Oppression is bearable, but unacceptable. Anyone who has tried to take action against it has made no mistake. Three attempts have failed; the seventh will succeed. The player records that he has lost a game. He did what he could. He reexamines his methods; he shows no contrition.

A SOBER ELITE

The Hungarian people are a fundamentally conservative people, and Hungarian culture is fundamentally a conservative culture. We came from far away in search of pasture and arrived here, on this lovely but stormy ground. It was hard for the nomads to settle down, hard to build cities, hard to become Christians; in many respects, we are pagans even today.

We are a lowland people, a people of the plains; we see as far as the eye can reach, we scan with suspicion anything that appears on the horizon, as if it were more likely to take from us than give to us. We were never a seafaring people, drawn by way of navigation into commerce; we only drove our fattened cattle to the West, like cowboys, and from there we brought everything that was more complex, more sophisticated, more polished. We are a sober people; our eyes see a long way off—every wellhead, every stork can be seen clearly in the distance. We have no forest elves, only hard-riding shamans. There is more fatalism in our mythology than terror and awe.

In my childhood the culture of the peasants was still intact. High culture, national culture, state culture was less pervasive than local popular culture, and the villages were more populous than the cities. (The cities were more noble

and military than bourgeois; the bourgeoisie was more Jewish and German than Hungarian.) These awkward, unedu-
cated peasants were thrust into two world wars from which
they had precious little to gain.

After World War II, under communist leadership, the
process of embourgeoisement received its greatest impetus.
This was something that neither the communists nor their
adversaries expected. Once again, history's basic long-term
processes fooled the short-lived, posturing actors, bemused
by their own words. Everyone knew that the communists
were against the bourgeoisie, and that was how they started
out. That *they* should be the ones to carry through the
process of embourgeoisement! It should bring a smile to the
historian's lips.

A stiff-necked people wants to regain its consciousness. It
has been a thousand years since a pastoral people with a
shamanistic religion accepted Chrisitianity, at considerable
pain, so they could have a king with a crown sent by the
Pope, and others would not regard them as a pack of
brigands.

Anyone who looks at a topographical map of Europe will
be struck by the geographical logic of the Carpathian basin,
its aesthetic attractiveness and natural unity. Once arrived
there, the Magyars absorbed the peoples they found in place
and many newcomers as well—Slavs, Cumans, Pechenegs,
Tartars, Turks, Germans, Romanians, Armenians, Jews—
though not entirely and not without difficulty; at times the
assimilating Magyar element was attenuated almost to the
point of extinction.

But in the end it survived, though not always with its

independence completely intact; it was sometimes subjected
to larger empires, fitted into their structure or attached to
them as a satellite. For a thousand years the Hungarian state
was able to function with relative autonomy, however, at
once the defender and oppressor of its people. The Magyars
seemed to show greater success in organizing an effective
state than other Eastern European peoples did.

The three medieval kingdoms of East Central Europe—
Polish, Czech, and Hungarian—seem to have been the work
of peoples who had great powers of survival. In one way or
another they paid dearly for their independence. Even
though the centuries-old experiment in independence has
still not reached a successful conclusion, this continuing
tenacity is proof that the struggle for self-determination will
go on until self-determination has been achieved.

It would be unhistorical folly to think that the Hungarian people, for example, after shaking off the rule of so
many other powers, will finally sink into resignation and
never take any action against its present and future occupiers. The Hungarian nation, like others, will not rest
until it has won self-determination here in the Carpathian
basin. Hungarians would like to regard every neighbor of
theirs with friendly strength, neither subjecting them nor
becoming subject to them, but working with them in natural exchange and cooperation.

It should be noted that this quite simple set of ideas—so
essential, if we are to have a healthy national strategy—has
frequently been obscured in our century by all kinds of
confused and tortuous reasoning. High culture has clouded
the mind of this sober people at least as much as it has
clarified it.

Throughout Hungarian history, our main aspiration has been a Hungarian state. If not a kingdom, then at least a principality; if not all of historic Hungary, then at least Transylvania; if not the whole Carpathian basin, then at least the center of it. If not complete independence, at least a limited independence. We joined with the Turks, we joined with the Germans, we joined with the Russians—not wholly as we would have liked, but never completely against our will either. If independence was qualified, at least there would be a Hungarian state. Hungarian could be spoken where Hungarians lived, Hungarians could carry out the business of governing them. If they didn't do so with perfect wisdom and skill, at least they were able to show some understanding and good will. We may get angry at our state and consider it unjust, but we want it to exist.

And we don't want it to be trampled in the dust, as it was in 1944–45. To be sure, that was the year of liberation, but it was also the year of the collapse of the historic Hungarian state. That event was at least as much a cause for bitterness as for joy. It would have been better if the historic Hungarian state had proven sufficiently intelligent, courageous, and skillful to avoid collapse.

Historical development is more than just a destiny, it is a responsibility as well. It is primarily the responsibility of the national elite, and within it of those thinking people who are considered the most intelligent and who are listened to most readily. Whenever some great national defeat occurs, we can surely say that those who should have risen to the occasion were not intelligent, courageous, and skillful enough. History is a continuous qualifying examination for the national elite.

The Magyars accepted the supremacy of the Christian state only with the greatest difficulty, and in the late Middle Ages they were unable to make the sacrifices necessary to preserve the national monarchy. Time and again, the Hungarian ruling elite placed its own narrow interests above the strategic interests of the Hungarian state and Hungarian national existence. The year 1944–45 was a fiasco because the prewar Hungarian elite was unable to formulate its own interests clearly and forthrightly, much less those of the country. Those prewar thinkers who were influential were also responsible for it. The responsibility for the future of our country weighs on our national elite today.

I find today's Hungarian elite more realistic than the prewar one. It cannot be said of them that they are altogether lacking in intelligence, courage, and skill. I think I can say, without risk of special pleading, that of all the countries of the Soviet bloc, Hungary is the one where the labors of the elite have proved most successful, hence most intelligent. A more thorough examination would not find that today's Hungarian political, economic, and cultural elite has any distinct, pronounced special interests that permanently conflict with the strategic interests of preserving the Hungarian state. And that is all the more true because its own interests have not yet congealed; they are still fuzzy, still in flux. Internal debate is still progressing and the results are only now beginning to be formulated.

Today's Hungarian elite has a grass-roots intuition when it comes to sensing the needs of state and people. A new middle class risen from the people is in the saddle and, while it doesn't want the impossible, it still wants a great deal. Our party cadres are made up today of people who yesterday might have been prosperous peasant farmers, craftsmen, and merchants—the same active, enterprising spirits who scramble their way to the top in any system. The most vigorous, clever, and persistent of our upward-striving workers and peasants have risen to become a state-socialist middle class, making their way through various channels of upward mobility, sometimes in political posts, at other times as technical staff or entrepreneurs (most often connected with state agencies).

An agrarian-industrial society with its own family temper and suppleness has grown up around the more militarized Soviet model of modernization. The members of today's Hungarian leadership elite are not dedicated ideologues or Marxist-Leninist world revolutionaries; they are the heirs of the process of embourgeoisement in Hungary. They represent the poor of yesteryear; their religion is growth; they have traveled much the same path as the bourgeoisie once did, albeit in a different way.

The character of the Eastern European elite is determined by the first generation of intellectuals with popular roots. They are still too ill at ease in their new roles to act grand; they look with the little man's suspicion on anything out of the ordinary. Their behavior is characterized by peasant shrewdness rather than lordly pride. This stratum genuinely prefers the security of the state to the uncertainties of competition. Venturesomeness had no part in their education. If, in order to rise, one has to go along rather than stand out, they can honestly and unashamedly go along. The streets are full of peasants dressed in city clothes.

The awkwardness and warmth of their origins is still upon
them. We have village-like cities and a family-like village-
state. Everybody knows everybody else. With its intimacy,
humor, and slyness, it is more a community than a society.
The clever ones pretend to be a little stupider than they
really are in order to make a niche for themselves. These
intellectuals from the people, be they poets or politicians,
resemble one another by reason of their origins. That is why
they can communicate so well with one another, even without saying everything right out.

This leadership elite is no more selfish and no stupider
than the prewar elite. It is less arrogant, friendlier, more
restrained, and more modest. It finds no particular difficulty
fitting into a state-socialist system; thanks to that system,
indeed, it has risen to the rank of an intellectual middle
class. Now that it has found a comfortable place for itself in
the world, this stratum has begun to demand more pluralism, but not so abruptly as to jeopardize its security. The
exceptional talents in its ranks have a difficult road, but the
middling sort seldom come into conflict with the censorship.
The regime, on the whole, allows as much aberration as the
average spirit is capable of.

The thinking of this first middle-class generation drawn
from the wide reaches of the people is not altogether adult;
it is rather respectful of authority and rather prejudiced. Its
criticisms are moral, not intellectual. Commanding and
obeying are more characteristic of its behavior than negotiation and compromise. Its manner of speaking is judg-
mental rather than relativistic. Its aesthetic views are
conservative rather than radical. Hesitant children, unsure
of themselves, fathers ill at ease—even the wily king-father

himself is an insecure provincial craftsman. Circumlocution is honest, outspokenness is decadent.

During World War II those who sided with the Germans did so from ideological conviction; today those who are pro-Russian heed a prudent recognition of reality. This is no alliance of enthusiasts; it is more like the tortuous agreements we used to make long ago with the Turks. Left to our own inclinations, we turn more to the West than the East. But the Turkish host was here for five hundred years, and now the Russian army is here. It came here not only in 1945 but also in 1956, at a time when it seemed that it was leaving and when the ambassador, Mr. Andropov, had promised that the troops would withdraw. Mr. Andropov, who no doubt entertains many different thoughts about this episode, certainly knew that the troops wouldn't leave—not just like that, leaving a defeat behind them. He acted as a consistent representative of the interests of a great power when he negotiated with Imre Nagy's government over the solemn formalities of the Soviet troop withdrawal. And he acted in the same capacity after the invasion of November 4, when he offered his counsel to János Kádár, Khrushchev's and Tito's choice to be the new Party secretary and premier.

We can probably agree that people may have different views of this affair. In December 1956, when the leaders of the workers' councils told him they had the people behind them, Kádár is supposed to have replied that he had the Soviet tanks behind him. We will not know for a long time yet the precise details of how Kádár came to find himself in that position and how much it represented his heart's desire. Some say he had to choose between taking on the premiership or going on trial and perhaps even to the scaffold. In any case, he was told that the Russians were coming. They were coming no matter what, and the only question was whose head the crown would come to rest upon. Perhaps he took it voluntarily, perhaps he was compelled to do it; in any event he must have known that he wasn't receiving it from the Hungarian people. He knew that this time the people weren't choosing their ruler and that his task would be to break the stubborn Hungarian nation to the Yalta system. Once there was order and obedience, he could try little by little to gain his countrymen's forgiveness, perhaps even their trust.

I don't know if János Kádár has read Machiavelli's *Prince*, but after 1956 that little masterpiece was my own constant companion. It told me what was coming next; it helped me understand the new leaders and the relatively young man (Kádár was then forty-four) who, of all his Eastern European peers, had best learned the role of the good prince. He had learned that power can be benevolent only if it is really *there*, indisputably and unequivocally; that only a secure regime can be humane; and that if it is secure, it will be humane. Kádár no doubt thought he could do things better than Rákosi, which wasn't hard; indeed, he probably hoped he could do better than most. Could it have been done better? From his point of view, probably not. In the tavern I hear, "God watch over Jani!" and "We'll be all right as long as he's in charge!" At one time verbal criticism of him figured frequently as one of the charges in antistate agitation trials, like *lèse majesté* in earlier times. Recently, in the village tavern that I frequent, a drunk went up to the policeman who drives out to the village once a week and, having nothing else to do, stops for a glass of beer. "Son," said the drunk, "you know where your Kádár can go? He can go to hell!" The drunk waited for the reaction. "Leave me alone," the policeman said. "Can't a man drink a beer in peace?" The bystanders laughed. The policeman drove off, and for another week the village was without armed authority, which it gets along without very well.

To this day, we don't know how many people besides Imre Nagy, Kádár's onetime colleague, were executed by the regime. Those who were in prison after 1956 say nearly two thousand; semiofficially, the figure given is five hundred. Even today historians are forbidden to investigate these facts. Even today the site of the graves of Imre Nagy and his companions is secret.

In the four-party government formed on November 1, 1956, there were three communist ministers: Imre Nagy (premier), János Kádár, and Géza Losonczy. At their trial in 1951, when the communists who had returned from Moscow after spending the war and early postwar years in the Soviet Union, settled accounts with the domestic communists, Kádár was first among the defendants and Losonczy was second. Both were tortured; their names are linked in history. Following the Russian intervention, Losonczy too was recommended for a post in the Kádár government; he refused. Either a minister or a prisoner—the choice was clear. He died while awaiting trial—following a hunger strike and forced feeding, when the food went into his windpipe and blocked it, according to one version. (In this country there are commonly several versions of historical fact.) After she grew up, Losonczy's daughter could have asked almost anything of her father's onetime friends in the highest leadership. She asked them to tell her where her father was buried. Ask anything, they said, but not that. Every year on the same day she went to Party headquarters and asked again. They never told her.

But it wasn't just the politicians, the professionals of power, who were involved. In the fall of 1959, when I was a welfare caseworker, my business took me one sunny afternoon to Százház Street (partly demolished since). If ever there was a slum, this was it—not just for dilapidation, poverty, and overcrowding, but also in its warmth and openness. Everyone knew everyone else; the residents lived out on the street. As I arrived there, I heard sobbing from all sides. What had happened? The next of kin of eighteen young men and one young woman had been notified that day to come to the central prison to pick up the young people's clothing. The nineteen had been hanged. They had been rebels in 1956, minors for the most part, street kids who had blown up several Soviet tanks. If they had been, for example, Algerians (the FLN was then fighting against the French), we might have been able to call them heroes. As it was, they were counterrevolutionary bandits. In the spring of 1959 the police blocked off the street and, going from house to house, arrested seventy young people; nineteen were later condemned to death. The reckoning was not a gentle one; they tried to put the best face on it by waiting until there were no longer any minors among the nineteen. No one knows who passed judgment on them and where. Not in Moscow, I don't think. Their petition for clemency may not even have reached Kádár. I would think, though, it was in his power to find out about it. This little episode is not recorded anywhere. Our written history is still being supplemented by oral tradition. In sum, the idyll began with reprisals of the classic type, and not just against those who rose in arms. I had to see a young widow whose children had run away. "How did your husband die?" I asked. "They hanged him," she replied. He was the chairman of a mineworkers' council; he didn't even own a pistol.

This is a bizarre kind of tradition of ours: an ugly beginning and a rather more appealing sequel. In 1920 Admiral Horthy* characterized his assumption of power as a counterrevolution; several hundred died and the prisons were full. (True, the "Lenin boys" with their leather coats and armored trains, who didn't have any compunctions about calling themselves the Red Terror, had likewise claimed several hundred summary victims.)

Afterward the Hungarians began to make their peace with Horthy, with the same conciliatory spirit they had shown previously toward Franz Josef, who also began by leading a counterrevolution. After the iron fist came the proffered hand. Liberalism followed, and consolidation, and that child of compromise, the idea of reform. But then World War II came with its uncertain prospect. Horthy would have liked to take Hungary out of the war, but he muffed the chance until it was too late. He wanted to emerge from the war with his own authority and that of his government intact more than he wanted to preserve the Hungarian state.

Our governments have confused themselves with the state, and their own interests with the interests of the whole

---

* The Naval officer and conservative leader who came to power following the defeat of revolutionary forces in Hungary after World War I and went on to become head of state from 1920 to 1944. [Publisher's note.]

population. They were unable to conceive of a legal transfer of power. When they collapsed as a result of their inadequate vision, their fall brought the country as well to a state of collapse.

World War II decimated the Hungarians, resulting in the death of half a million Christians and half a million Jews. To stay out of the war was impossible, of course; if Hungary had not entered the war on the German side, Hitler's troops would most likely have occupied the country. The Jews would have been deported even sooner. There would still have been a compliant government to send soldiers to the front. There would still have been bombings, and the battlefront would still have passed over us. The Russians would still have been our liberators, and we would still have passed from the German sphere of influence to the Russian.

The line between wisdom and error is very thin. Here and there, perhaps, it might have been possible to reduce the number of victims. In our part of the world, wise policies are not always rewarded with social and national freedom. Sometimes the most that wise policies can accomplish here is to minimize the amount of tangible and intangible sacrifice.

The state can be the protector of society and can serve to articulate its interests; indeed, those things are its business. Some officials are stupid, but stupidity is not the statistical norm. Many pliant opportunists join the Party, but forceful personalities also join, in order to find a field for their energies. Could all this have been done better? Certainly. The Kádárist ruling stratum could itself have understood sooner and more clearly just what it was doing. It might have been possible for open thinking to get started on the margins of society sooner. It might have been possible for the main body of the intelligentsia to begin discussing the universal sentiment for reform sooner. It might have been possible to carry through the economic reform more vigorously and without stopping short for long, costly years during the 1970s.

The Hungarian intelligentsia and the Hungarian middle class have never formulated, much less discussed, what sort of world view might be appropriate to our situation in the world and potentially useful in both the short and long run. We have not thought through what we want. We have not discussed what we wish to do with our opportunities. We have not arrived at any conscious self-awareness. Naturally we want external independence and internal democracy, so far as possible. But how far is it possible? Just this far, or farther than this? It's our own fault that we weren't smarter than we were. Individuals can be more independent than their government. We could be freer, better educated, and more clear-sighted than we are.

Planning and monitoring our future course is the business of the intelligentsia. It is the business not only of the official intelligentsia for whom it is difficult to speak freely, but also of opposition intellectuals who are willing to undertake the adventure of speaking openly, even at the risk of being excluded from the official world and the tacit consensus.

We can progress further along the "Hungarian road" only if, by getting to know ourselves and the terrain around us better, we become clear about where we are headed and what vicissitudes await us. Everybody—government supporters and oppositionists alike—is moving together along the same road. Some would like to go more in this direction, others more in that one. Some want to go faster, others slower. Everyone governs a little, even if he governs no one but himself.

Often it seems to me that the leaders themselves are just feeling their way. Perhaps they can see farther ahead by instinct, but in any case they long ago gave up believing that the future would turn out the way they had planned. They are happy if they can muddle through the day-to-day difficulties. With any luck they no longer see mortal enemies in those who, unburdened by the cares of office, go on sounding off about the right course to follow.

This regime can strike hard, yet for a long time now it hasn't. It seems not to hear the occasional admonition from outside to be more strict. It acts rather like a lenient teacher who never raises his voice in an unruly classroom except when he sees the principal coming. The children know there really isn't much to be afraid of. They see the principal coming, too, and they know he'll go away again. Before long they will be left alone with the soft-hearted teacher, who would like to have order but has no taste for cracking the whip.

It is possible to minimize the cost to our country of our remaining on the eastern side of the Iron Curtain, with the consent of the Western powers, and of our contributing, precisely by reason of our limited sovereignty, to the maintenance of the international military balance. But our contribution to European peace is that we are trying to take our modicum of self-determination—limited, but still better than nothing and capable of being expanded modestly—and give it, through cautious experimentation, a living content.

To ask for a regime very different from the one we have now is impossible. And would it be desirable? One could say a lot about that. I for my part simply take note that a Hungarian road and a Hungarian style of government have evolved within the structure of Yalta, something we can now speak of as Kádárism, though only in retrospect, looking back over the past quarter of a century.

The man who has given his name to this social situation has now been in power for twenty-five years. He has managed to avoid being overthrown or killed, and also the unscrupulous excesses that can come with the intoxication of power. He gave scope to men around him who were sober and moderate like himself, if not particularly brilliant. He knew how to act with paternal dignity on the stage of a society which in its bones has never been averse to paternalism. In our popular legend he has come, perhaps, to occupy a place comparable to that of our king Franz Josef, who mercilessly crushed the Hungarian people's struggle for independence in 1849 with Russian help, then went on to rule by the grace of God for sixty-seven years and in the meantime sealed a constitutional compromise with us, opening the way to an era of rapid development. Everyone grew used to the idea of the old man sitting in his Spartan workroom, an image that would be remembered even more fondly if in the end he had not led his people, quite deliberately, into world war.

Every Hungarian government has to avoid two pitfalls—arousing the wrath of Moscow and arousing the wrath of Hungarian society. In mediating between Moscow and the Hungarians our government strives to pacify both. We would like to see it try to please Hungarian society a little more, without aggravating Moscow. We wouldn't like to see the imperial center come to regard us as a focal point of tension that ought to be put down. If we were to attract its vigilant anger, the pressure on us afterward would be heavier than before. But it's all right if, from time to time, rumblings of disapproval reach us from the court of the Sultan or the Emperor. If there were no differences of interest or opinion, how would it be possible to bargain at all?

We ought to avoid becoming a major theater of operations for the world's communications media. It is not in our interest to have a legion of correspondents busy sharpening our differences. If there is too much press attention on us, we will wind up talking not to the issues, not to our patron or our friends, but to an international audience hungry for sensation. International public opinion's approval and disapproval alike are transient things, matters of fashion; when things come to a head, it cannot be counted on. International public opinion could not save our fighters from prison and the scaffold. In our calculations, then, we should accord the foreign media only a limited role, as auxiliaries in our enterprise.

It is the domestic game that is most important. In today's world, most political events have the potential to become shows that run for weeks or months. If the actors have any histrionic inclinations, they can enter the mythology of the media for a time, but their sense of dramatic importance jeopardizes the chances of slow and steady progress; it catches up our local affairs in the struggle between the two power blocs and deprives conflict management of the ironic complicity that normally exists between the partners in the purely domestic game.

Since we cannot openly be either contractual allies or a sharply defined opposition, we must be reformists, critical players for democracy against those who play to defend the Party-state's monopoly of power. We must be their opponents in behalf of democracy, and at the same time their collaborators in behalf of undisturbed national survival.

We who labor for autonomy will do well if we can make the foreign press and radio our instrument, without letting ourselves become an instrument of theirs. In the eyes of the Yalta system, the free expression of our national and human interests is a subversive act. Power and world public opinion have a paradoxical community of interest: both see in autonomous words and deeds a crime, a challenge, a deviation, a heresy, an emotional and hence theatrical provocation.

In this kind of situation I don't consider it demeaning for the Hungarian intelligentsia to regard itself as one great conspiracy of scoundrels. We know this attitude from centuries of our history, and are capable of distinguishing nicely between bargaining and betrayal. We don't condemn our Transylvanian princes, closely pressed by German and Turkish power, for their two-faced, tongue-in-cheek maneuvers. If the Russian leaders attribute emotional importance to symbols, then let us, our Party, and our government leaders treat their symbols gently. A Hungarian patriot can commit no more foolish act than to deface a Soviet military memorial. I like that Hungarian village where the memorials to the Soviet and Hungarian war dead are combined in one, on which the following is written: "Pause here, stranger, before this memorial to the soldiers who fell on the edge of our village." Let this example of village shrewdness stand as a symbolic expression of the Hungarian road.

A nation's wisdom is most clearly seen in the way it deals with risk. It should try to gauge where the greatest advantage lies at the least possible risk. Risk has no value of its own, but at times we may need to anticipate danger and take a bold step first. We will be able to take that step at the best possible moment and with the greatest assurance only if our style of play in general has been one that avoids risks.

To play for victory—to offer up less of our blood and passion and more of our brains and labor—that would truly be a new strategy for a nation whose history is marked by so many defeats because it was too cowardly on some occasions and unwarrantably daring on others.

THE HUNGARIAN ROAD

Our real mood is one of neither victory nor defeat, but of experimentation. When I look around I see that everyone is starting something, planning, trying his skills, telling of some small success. It may be an experimental school, an interesting research project, a new orchestra, a publishing opportunity, a screenplay accepted, a little restaurant about to open, an association of mathematicians, an attractive private shop, a private gallery, a trip to the West, cultural undertakings, independent publications, semiunderground journals.

Alongside the second economy a second culture is coming into style which may stimulate and enliven the officially accepted culture, whose own boundaries, if not exactly open, are at least not so terribly closed as they once were. Many things are possible now, many things are allowed—but not everything, of course. There is a slow expansion of the limits. An honest documentary appears on TV, a good serious play at one of the theaters, an interesting study in a periodical. Official quarters are gradually taking cognizance of reality in both economy and culture. They are also becoming aware of the real system of values, that of the market and of undirected public opinion.

Hungarian society is beginning to resemble us. The ideas that come into our heads today will be common coin tomorrow. We are not much smarter than we appear to be through the veil of censorship. Official culture is not much stupider than we are. There is no sharp break between culture and reality, only some displacement. We are not exactly winners, but the stereotype of a nation in decline—that threadbare product of a mournful romanticism—doesn't fit us either. We are a society approaching the threshold of maturity, beginning to lift its head, beginning to conduct a dialogue with itself. Even socialist reform thinking has a twenty-year history.

Wherever we stand, we are all Hungarians, all members of the team, all part of this Hungarian reality, as they call it. We are all actors in the same play. Ten million roles and ten million outlooks, on various levels of profundity, imagination, and experience. The whole production was thrown together somehow. The performance is not absolutely first-rate, but it is still worth watching.

The essence of the Hungarian road is the emergence of a certain limited pluralism within the confines of the Yalta system. This limited pluralism doesn't reflect any weakness on the part of the system; on the contrary, it is a sign of its strength. The system is now capable of absorbing and integrating undertakings that not so long ago were disowned or hushed up. It can openly acknowledge the existence of certain structural conflicts. It no longer considers it a life-or-death matter to cloak reality in ready-made images. Heretics, practitioners of black magic, bearded alchemists dripping brimstone are stirring the state's orthodox clerics to meditation and dialogue.

This is not yet postconciliar socialism, but the theses of the council are cropping up. Everywhere in society there is a greater readiness to exchange ideas. The leaders themselves are not immune to the spirit of an objectivity that goes to the heart of things. Intellectual novelties circulate with increasing velocity. When those who write outside the censorship produce work that is original as well as courageous, everyone soon knows about it. We are in touch with one another. The censorship toils conscientiously, but has come to recognize that the government can tolerate a brisker traffic in information without beginning to totter. The system has more self-confidence, and that is a good thing for us.

There is no national highroad of history, alongside which the paths other nations have followed are only side roads. The less we think there is a single highroad, the more interesting our own road becomes. The Soviet road is not the highroad, of course; just now I saw on television that the Soviets are reorganizing the management of their agricultural system so there will be enough potatoes. Communism: lots of tanks, too few potatoes. Lots of pretensions, too few results. What kind of a highroad is that? And of course the American road is not the highroad either, nor is the Japanese, the German, the French, the Swedish, or any other road. There are no standard models, no exemplary systems.

There are so many kinds of goals to strive for, so many kinds of successes to console ourselves with! Every community sets itself a different set of goals. In the sphere of culture, if anywhere, progress has been and remains uneven. Culture doesn't wax and wane in proportion to economic growth. We can excel there even if we are not so very numerous or rich or menacing. The fact that we live in a small country doesn't place us at any disadvantage in trying to understand ourselves and explore the fundamental questions of life. Jerusalem and Athens, Florence and Amsterdam were smaller cities than Budapest.

If there is one area of human activity in which unexpected advances and declines may occur, it is the realm of cultural creativity. Today, it seems to me, Budapest could become for Soviet-dominated Central Europe what Vienna was for Central Europe at the turn of the century. We went under and we came back up again. In the middle of our tunneling we hear voices from the other side. We have broken through the great simplification. Sensing the complexity of a mature Europe, we smile at one another. Today, it almost seems that we are not at the mercy of some impending folly any longer. It almost seems that we are not about to lose our way again willfully.

There is censorship in Hungary, of course, just as there is in the other communist countries, but the Hungarian censorship is less narrow, more openminded and lenient. We could perhaps say that of all the countries of the Soviet bloc, Hungary has the mildest censorship, and so here one has the least to fear from the state. This makes people's social and written contacts with others relatively lively; one can take part in interesting discussions, read good books, get hold of Western newspapers and magazines. Hungarian-language radio broadcasts from the West are not jammed. Hungarian citizens have a legal right to apply for a passport to visit the West, and the government may issue one if it sees fit (it is not obliged to do so). The great majority of applicants receive permission to travel to the West once a year.

We almost—but only almost—live under a government of laws. There are limits to openness, limits to freedom, but there's no tight totalitarian control. Here, the people who call the government totalitarian are the ones looking for an excuse for their own cautious accommodation to the censorship. If anyone tries to exercise freedom of thought and finds that it demands a price (though not a fatal one), he ought to regard his remaining at liberty as proof that the system we live under is not the absolute antithesis of democracy.

If a young person wants to succeed, it will do him no harm to become active in the Young Communist League, join the

Party, and enroll in one of the evening schools of Marxism-Leninism; he will sacrifice many advantages and incur many disadvantages if he prefers the pleasures of thinking freely to the goods available from the state, the better jobs and higher pay, the house obtainable with government help on favorable terms, the frequent trips abroad at state expense, the chance to play a part in public life.

Naturally, most people want to succeed, and Western observers should be the last ones to wonder at that. Making good is a chancier business here, and more suspect than in the West. Still, there is a minority—as there always must be—who prefer to be on good terms with themselves rather than with the state. They pay for this singular friendship with their careers. You can't have it all.

What is and what is not allowed in Hungary today? Thinking is allowed. Thinking for yourself seldom entails any unpleasant consequences; if it does, they can be lived through without any serious damage. These unpleasant consequences can even have an incentive effect: they spur one on to freer thinking. Who knows how much more intelligent the country would be if it were free to be intelligent, if there were no political repression at all?

When people cannot express something in one form, they express it in another. To understand a country is to examine what its inhabitants have had to give up, and what they have compensated themselves with in return for their sacrifice. What doesn't work for them, and what does work for them instead? What makes them, by and large, just as happy as the inhabitants of other countries? If the values that seem fundamental elsewhere are less powerful here, there must be others that the inhabitants of this country explicitly or implicitly consider primary.

It seems to me that Hungary doesn't excel in the kinds of accomplishments that can be measured by any competitive yardstick. In the global statistics of technical achievements we are seldom near the top. In this area we do better than some Eastern European countries, but in selling our products on the world market we are only average. We do better at those intangibles that one might call the art of living: the cultivation of domestic comfort; an easygoing way of life; the art of getting on with one another; a certain worldly wisdom and a certain distance toward things that others consider vitally important; a healthy, pagan cynicism toward dedicated fanatics. It is as rewarding to sit in a well-kept garden at twilight drinking a quiet glass of wine with friends as it is to tear along a crowded eight-lane highway.

In Hungary, it is not possible to criticize the political structure—the upper level organs and leaders of the Party and state—plainly and systematically, without euphemism, in the public media. Lower ranking agencies and officials can be subjected to a didactic and moral criticism. The phenomena of economic life can also be criticized, independently of the people and institutions responsible for them; however, the Party leadership, the ministries, and the police don't tolerate criticism.

It is quite impossible for anyone to advocate a referendum on the three great questions that are decisive for our national and social self-determination. First: should we remain a member of the Warsaw Pact military alliance? Second: should we choose our parliamentary representative from the candidates of one party or several? Third: should the directors of our productive enterprises be chosen by the authorities or by bodies elected by the workers? It is quite impossible to publish factual information about the censorship in the officially licensed press, only in *samizdat* publications. The first level of censorship is the most immediate: self-censorship. Next comes the cultural apparatus, including the whole hierarchy of editors and Party and ministerial functionaries. Finally there is the political police, which watches the citizenry, admonishes them, regularly consults with their superiors about them and advises on their advancement, and which goes on working quite effectively even if no one is arrested for thinking whatever he wants. At least educated people are not arrested; unknown young workers occasionally are.

It is not possible to subject to any objective scrutiny the criminal justice system, the prisons, the far-flung network of interrogations and mail censorship; or the archaic custom of confiscating books objectionable to the state from citizens at the frontier; or the oppressively widespread practice of inducing a great many people who deserve better to inform on their associates—persuading these informers by means of intimidation, money, promotions, or other favors and thereby converting them into moral zombies.

The system can get used to the existence of a house where people can pick up uncensored writings in mimeographed form. The reflex that sees every divergent opinion as hostile and hence punishable, works ever more intermittently. For the time being, it seems, the police have not been directed to get rid of the second culture, only to keep it within

bounds. Now and then there are still confiscations or
lengthy and unpleasant surveillances; sometimes people involved in independent publishing are followed on the street
by a larger contingent of heavies than the prime minister is.
We turn to the public, we sign things, with deliberation and
moderation; our answers are considered and adroit.

It would be no more possible to wipe out the second
culture and still keep a liberal image in the world, than it
would be to restrict the economic autonomy of all the
entrepreneurs, large and small, and still maintain the standard of living. The government must learn—and is learning
—that there's a price to pay for keeping its good name. It is
impossible to strike a civilized pose before the world public
and at the same time apply heavy-handed police measures to
intimidate the few people who reject the censorship's base
ritual by refusing to cooperate in the game of "Oh, there's
no censorship here, I didn't really want to say any more
than I could get printed, not a word more."

This Hungarian experiment is a delicate game, easily
spoiled. Our old buggy is really beginning to roll. We sit
in it, waiting to see if it's going to crash, because that's what
it's usually done. Now it's time to sober up; we've brought
things as far as we could. Our situation is our self-portrait.
Fortune, misfortune—isn't that how fools talk? History isn't
made by some malevolent destiny; we make it ourselves,
according to our abilities. If it crosses us up again, it'll be
because we were not competent enough. Whenever I hear
historical necessity mentioned, or national misfortune, I
think of the dull schoolboy who "by chance" didn't know
the answer to the question he was being asked, no matter
what the question.

Of all the aspects of the critique of state society, the intellectuals' program for setting limits to the state is perhaps the most interesting. Their criticism becomes evident if, for example, one goes to a conference at a scholarly institute in Budapest where people from decision-making levels of the government are also present. The growing self-confidence of the scholarly intelligentsia toward the executive intelligentsia, and the subtlety and point of their arguments, can be felt in the discussion, in which representatives of the more conservative sectors of the regime are reduced to defending themselves indignantly (the most interesting part of the whole thing is that there are less conservative sectors of the regime, too).

The chances of limiting the state increase if it becomes possible for us intellectuals to survive apart from the state, without the goods that the state takes from the producers and gives to us. (Otherwise we would only be cutting off the limb we sit on, since the state is a daddy who gives us money, albeit not much.) So far, the economic autonomy of the organs of intellectual self-management has not really been tested. What would happen if they did acquire independence and succeeded in holding their own in the marketplace?

Greater independence with respect to redistributive centralism; a brisk circulation of freely associating and self-governing intellectual groups in the marketplace of ideas; alternative enterprises dedicated not to maximum profit but to intellectual activity for its own sake, to making a living without any urge to get rich; in short, an amalgam of the second economy and the second culture—that is the road that beckons to the ablest young intellectuals of Eastern Europe. It is perhaps the only way they can emancipate themselves, step by step, from the rhetoric and intellectual discipline of the state.

VICTORY OR PERSUASION?

Every one of us is a participant in the match between the state and creative intelligence; we are its medium and its material, and there is not one of us in whom the game has finally been decided one way or the other. The debate between power and creativity has an ontological character; it cannot but exist. It appears in multiparty political systems, too, because the intellectual transcendence of what exists is always essentially the work of a minority. But it is endemic in one-party states, where the authorities, having claimed for themselves a 99 percent majority, don't feel obliged to give any scope at all to the minority ideas that confront them.

In Eastern Europe this confrontation between informal spiritual authority and formal worldly authority is genuine theater; it is the most frequent subject of our dialogue. But there is no reason why this game between the intellectual elite and the power elite should be bitter and barbarous, even in those states of Eastern Europe where there is less room for maneuver. It can be a civilized and even sporting affair, relative to the level of political sophistication of the players. Each side ought to play on the ground where it is strongest. Authority feels most comfortable in the medium of favors and punishment, intellect in the medium of words and symbols. The more symbolic the game is, the more advanced it is.

The game is at its most elegant when the players are not embittered. The important thing is that what we are doing should be good. The present is a special time. Enjoying each hour is in itself a struggle for liberation. Why should I do evil for the sake of good? I don't have to wait until I'm free to be happy. Right now I am trying to become free, and I am happy. We have basic groundwork to do on ourselves, for we are still a long way from the self-government of our own persons. If we strive for a state of internal détente, a relaxation of spiritual tensions, then we will meet with defeat less often and the state will become less terrifying.

I am most likely to cultivate my freedom in the company of those I like. In organizations, too, small is beautiful; there one finds the solidarity of friends. I don't think I would ever want to name my circle of friends the National Association of Friends—much less the Hungarian State Association of Friends. I consider a network of informal circles of friends to be our natural form of organization. In large formal organizations either the parts pull the whole this way and that, or else a domineering minority—the central apparatus—imposes its authority on the parts. Those smaller, more easily encompassed circles are playing their own game. They add new gradations to the spectrum; they take responsibility for themselves and know how to make fine distinctions. I wish us the brightest good spirits, here and now. There is no need to wait for the distant triumph of our ideas. Friendship is everything; the final goal is a dream.

In Eastern Europe things are overdetermined, and it is a hefty challenge for us to pursue the adventure of self-determination. We will either slow down the workings of our minds or else start questioning everything. On nearly every issue, the nationalized intelligence leaves off just when things are beginning to get interesting. Nationalized prevarication comes in the guise of cliché, and its sorry consequence is that much of the debate carried on against it also takes the form of cliché. Issues which, a few hundred miles from here, have ceased to be issues—would they still preoccupy us if we didn't constantly have to deal with them from inside, rather than from outside and above? The bowed nationalized soul doesn't dare to straighten up. It is easy, he says, for those who walk tall; they selfishly throw off the weight that bows us all.

If I give up my freedom, I will waste away; the soul that is let out for hire is troubled and dark. Lying about anything is not permissible; after the three-quarter-truth comes the half-truth and then the quarter-truth. In a troubled culture, after so many twists and turns, there are no guidelines for lying any more. Self-censorship is self-stultification; it impairs our mental libido. If keeping still is ethical, then speaking out indiscreetly is the sweetest of sins.

Authoritarian nation-states are like our county administrations. But you don't have to stick it out in one of the more provincial counties, putting up with the indignities of the deputy county administrator. In a small-town culture, the topics of discussion are small-town. We eat a lot, we drink a lot; a fat man takes tiny steps. A poor country, a fat style—bulging, sentimental, clumsy.

International culture is everywhere at once now; the world is one, and it is more interesting than Budapest. Beginning steps: I am still too acceptable; I will try to free myself to be more unacceptable. In our cozy, somewhat deferential culture, you have to watch what you say lest you offend the people you're talking with. If a writer is afraid, his mind won't be on the words but on the consequences. Less fear is better: it means self-conquest and greater insight.

It is difficult to live properly and create something that didn't exist before—my own anticlichés. The iconography of agreement has to be constructed all over again. Who am I? What is all this here around me? A sleepwalker's progress, a crossroads every few minutes. You yourself are the furthest point. Utopia, not the past, is the foundation of autonomy.

In tight places we console ourselves with profundity. Who knows if it's really like this? It's a fact that prison diaries are not more interesting than picaresque novels. But it can also happen that a prisoner, after he has been questioned, enters into the game and begins to question himself; when that happens, his cell becomes a world stage. The man who is hard pressed seeks some secret source of strength and discovers his inner freedom. Along with that, he tries to respond by casting a sharp glance over the whole culture. To dispute what we are is an adventure on a par with suicide.

Autonomy is a kind of mystic paranoia. From the view-point of a conservative spirit, the radical soul is pathological. If you subject everything that is "human" to close examination, nothing is natural. The more freedom becomes an intimate companion, the more oppressive it can be, like an uninhabited island.

A thinker wins not when he takes over from his adversary but when he wins him over. A creator's success comes when men of power begin to see the world in the same way he does. It is possible to imagine a refined dialectic of research and execution as well. Creative thinking strives to define the ideas and the style that regulate a culture, including the political culture. Intellectual influence is an exercise of power.

If the intellectuals don't want to let their minds out for hire, they must go after their own power, which is neither military nor political nor economic, but cultural. There is a ripening awareness that it is more honest and effective for the intelligentsia to play its own game and to learn to take responsibility for its own peculiar sort of intangible power.

To what extent the participants focus their discussions on relevant questions depends on us. If the questions are muddled, the answers will be muddled. At least one of the players in the game ought to formulate them with precision. Yet it may happen that the whole spectrum of a nation's intelligentsia will miscalculate and build its strategy on unreal assumptions. The penalty for that comes when the game gets rough and finally the weapons come out. The power elite is not alone to blame for that; the fault may be the cultural elite's as well.

To replace a power elite with a shadow power elite is a waste. It is more productive, on the whole, for everyone to stay put and let the process of selection be gradual and individual. Frontal attacks with regular troops are to be avoided. Better that the contest be conducted like a knightly tournament, or better still like the battle of the sexes, which can be neither suspended nor centrally organized.

To impugn the power of the state is impolite on the one hand, while on the other it enrages those worthy souls who identify the power of the state with themselves. The question of who will be boss excites only those who consider being boss the highest earthly good. It is more important to take back from the censors the writing table you are sitting at. On its surface there is no room for lies.

Politics has grown fat; it has to be trimmed down. The political elite has overextended itself; overstepping its proper sphere of influence, it has meddled with things that are not its affair and neglected those tasks that properly fall within its province. Eavesdropping, grilling people, harassing them, putting all sorts of obstacles in their way—these are flaws of character (historically progressive flaws of character, to be sure, when the socialist state practices them). With bourgeois conservatism, I expect of the state that it should function as discreetly and efficiently as the water works or the national railways.

A paternalistic state society under the leadership of the intelligentsia is being consolidated here. It is going to have to carry out difficult reforms on an ever more mature level of political consciousness; it must consciously display a rational courage, bearing in mind that only a secure regime can execute courageous reforms.

Radical art and moderate policy can be reconciled, it seems to me, in such a way as to be intellectually productive. During the Hungarian reform era of the 1840s, how many responsible political positions were taken up between the two poles of radicalism and conservative liberalism! Today as well, it seems possible to have coordinated teamwork from master players with differing conceptions of the world.

If we employ a democratic style, we can make an advance payment on democracy. Theoretical discussion is inherently more dignified than power struggle. We can become an adult nation if we introduce ideological pluralism in preparation for the political pluralism that will come in due time. That much can be done even within the bounds of state society, by developing the art of clarifying and reconciling divergent and common interests.

A sophisticated, lucid, orderly, matter-of-fact, and good-natured politics is what I would like to see. I have no objection to politicians who are experienced and who have learned to control their anger. I expect that my representatives will be politicians schooled in power. I don't mind if they have worked their way up the ladder, demonstrating their abilities in small matters. If they are well trained, perhaps they will occupy their seats without feeling ill at ease. Perhaps they will avoid making much of the fact that power is theirs, just as a pianist avoids making much of the fact that the piano is his.

My kind of politician is a stranger to insecurity, conceit, feelings of inferiority, and heavyhandedness. When it's time to analyze an issue, he is able to avoid thinking of himself first. He doesn't hate with a passion anyone who disagrees with him. He respects the forms, the elaborate rituals. He doesn't stoop to the bad form of applying the moral lash to those who stand in his way.

I regard the upheavals of 1968 in France and elsewhere as essentially a cultural revolution, a rebellion of the young intelligentsia against their role as instruments. They rebelled against an existence in which the intellectual is a highly trained wage worker, a technical expert who, having sold his labor either grudgingly (as a value-free act) or willingly, finds himself performing tasks whose meaning and propriety he is not able (or even much inclined) to judge; who does what he is told and what he is paid for. The young people of 1968 didn't want to be respectable, established intellectual whores. They wanted to reclaim the meaning of their work. They insisted on the right to practice their occupations with an independent conscience. They were looking for the dignity of the intelligentsia.

The greatest failing of the movements of workers and intellectuals in 1968 was that they never succeeded in defining themselves in their own terms, only in terms of their supposed enemy, capitalism. Thus they blundered into communism, the religion of revolution. Once more the proletariat faded from sight behind the starving hundreds of millions of the Third World. Sympathizing with China, the movements became the plaything of Peking's political elite. Sympathizing with the PLO, they became the plaything of

Moscow's playthings. The Western intellectuals of 1968 thought a good deal more about who their adversaries were than about who they themselves were and what they wanted. After their revolutionary role had proven hollow, they finally regressed to a neoinfantile, psychoconsumerist culture which went comfortably with the normalization of their social role, leaving behind a few complexes and identity crises for purposes of conversation.

We Eastern Europeans have less freedom than Westerners, and hunger for it all the more. For that very reason, perhaps, we would like to go farther than they have in securing individual and collective liberties. If our aim is only to catch up with Westerners in the matter of freedom, as we have tried to do in technology, then of course we will never catch up with them at all.

People all over the world watched the Polish social movement attentively. Everyone who was thrilled to see a people turn with fresh vigor to social renewal became an expert on Poland, from afar, and went there, if at all possible, to look around and draw breath. For a year and a half Poland was the most interesting theater of the global drama. Now the Iron Curtain has been rung down again. In Poland the company is preparing underground for the next production. They hope to learn from the shortcomings of the last one. They have to rethink once again what it is that makes their enterprise special.

In our area the time has come for a kind of politics—or rather antipolitics, as I would call it—which doesn't just mean rising on the ladder of state office. It would not bring a better job, promotion, or jump in income. It would not bring an official car, a bodyguard, and a flock of secretaries. It would mean defending the place, the job, and the work we now have and want to keep. Antipolitics is not a dream of the future; it is respect for the present.

If an architect is an antipolitician, he will try to build better, according to his lights, with fewer constraints, rather than struggle up the official ladder to reach those offices where architects who don't design any more decide on the work of those who still do, generally only to make their work more difficult by burdening them with unnecessary regulations.

What is most important today, it seems to me, is to emancipate thinking people from the narrow vision of national teamwork under state auspices and to engage in a dialogue high above the level of governments and national boundaries. I would like to see each elite begin to clarify its interests and strategic aims in the international arena, weighing in a businesslike way what it can agree about with parties having other interests, and where it must exert pressure on others to bring them to concessions.

Indeed, there is a professional strategic elite emerging in both the superpowers that knows how to weigh matters rationally, avoid overreaction, provide balanced and pointed answers, and formulate with precision what it wants. The problem is that this elite makes itself heard too rarely. Its voice is drowned out by the turgid rhetoric and empty sensationalism of ideological war—a hollow bluff, not even fit to play poker with, much less international poker. The international intelligentsia needs a more lucid and less lurid public arena where we can tell one another more plainly what we want, abandoning the sleazy language of propaganda. There we could certainly play our games with and against one another with a good deal more imagination.

History is not in the first instance a tale of masters and men, oppressors and oppressed; it is a record of the struggles of elite groups competing for power. The majority can live with the rule of an established elite; they will turn away from one elite only if it has deceived them, and if they feel more confidence in another.

DEMOCRACY BEFORE SOCIALISM

Every culture has a grammar; ours does, and so do those of the other Europeans. How do we distill ourselves into a text, how does the text arise from our texture? There are occasional, local, conditional, and relative grammatical rules of communication. There are intercultural agreements, too, permanent and universal. Our moral history lies in our progress toward these rules, through a succession of errors. In the world of the philosophers, these agreements stand out. Geniuses don't all sing in the same chorus, but they understand one another better than the blinkered majority who are prey to misunderstanding, to taking offense, and to squabbling. These rules together make up a methodology of social communication.

Our experience is that the undisturbed communication of metaphysically equal subjects is best assured by a carefully cultivated mutual respect. Liberal philosophy expresses with the greatest formal coherence our European culture's most considered agreements on how we should harmonize our interests. Such philosophy finds its social and political form in democracy. Liberalism is much more than the propaganda of those political parties that call upon its name. Liberalism is a political mentality mindful of the mutually acceptable rules of the game and how to develop them. It means intellectual rigor and an insistence on fair play. That is where the significance of liberalism is to be found, as well as the case for it.

Children who can't read yet can argue about what's all right in a game and what isn't all right, what's fair and what's not fair. Consciously or not, every sports fan shares a philosophy of fair play. Liberal democracy has no need to repress people's expression of their spontaneous sense of justice, or their debates about whether a given measure is a fair rule of the game, because such debates and corrections only make the system stronger. Dictatorship, on the other hand, is incorrigible in this respect. If it doesn't repress the free discussion of legislation, it will be overthrown by law. Liberal philosophy creates stability; antiliberal philosophies produce instability.

Democracy has its own style, which follows from a strategy of learning. A learner believes it is more important to learn than to teach. Sensing how little is known of all the things that could be known, he is ironic; he sees that the unknown is the greater part. The heroes of the European intelligentsia have been learners and not teachers, experimenters rather than defenders of existing knowledge. A society that learns is the root idea of all utopias—a community of people living together according to wise ordinances, constantly reviewing and refining them, with thoroughness and care.

It is nonsense to suppose that any utopia would approve of censorship. A utopian society is one that has become a subject for itself, through free communication among personalities open to learning. By definition, society is self-shaping and experimental, since it is made up of individual human beings with wills of their own, and there is no commandment sent from some higher sphere that is superior to their will. All existing rules are human, devised by human beings, demanded and observed by them. Our rules cannot be directly derived from any hypothesis about God or history. They are our work, and if we don't like them we can make others instead. If a small group of people clings by force to rules that the majority accepts only under compulsion, sooner or later revolutions will breach those rules and alter them radically.

Real reform is possible only in liberal democracies, where the majority, after hearing out the views of the minority, can act to change the laws. In dictatorships, reform is pseudoreform—a softening of the dictatorship, a lifting of this or that onerous restriction forced on the majority, while at the same time the overall system of restraints and prohibitions imposed by the minority remains in force.

Human beings are in principle free with respect to one another, since they can either kill or come to terms with one another. Dictatorship doesn't really exist, even if it goes on for a long time, because it is so chancy. Anyone can kill the dictator. No one knows in advance who may become a tyrannicide. The wisest and most powerful tyrant cannot see into the mind of his most wretched and dull-witted servant. Hitlerism would have collapsed if the attempt on Hitler's life had succeeded. The constitutional democracy of the United States, on the other hand, remains undisturbed by the assassination of Presidents.

A society is more advanced the more it becomes a subject for itself, the more conscious it becomes of its own interests. Limited autonomy means a cruder culture, a society of people who are not much given to thinking. Where individuals are not free, society is not free either. If the individuals in socialist society are not free, socialism is not a society of freedom. It represents something cruder: a dictatorship in the face of which revolution is justified.

In a liberal democracy, socialist reforms can be adopted by parliamentary majority, according to the constitutional rules of the game. Democracy is more important and more basic than the reform of income and property relations. Democracy can include socialism, but one-party state socialism cannot include democracy. If it gives ground, citizens newly awakened to their dignity will destroy the rigidly centralized political structure.

A socialism that benefits the majority—whether by the just redistribution of income or by the just redistribution of power—is possible only in a society where the majority decides and the minority is free to voice its opinion without restriction. If the so-called achievements of socialism cannot be debated there is no democracy. It is a cardinal principle that the values of democracy precede those of socialism (while in no way denying them).

The political, artistic, and scientific avant-garde is the

creation of learners, people who recognize neglected human possibilities. Tradition is a product of learning, but so too is the radical demand that action be justified not merely by images of the past but also by images that speak of an imagined future. The past has not been so wonderful as to make utopia superfluous.

It is a false learning model that ranks what each of us has learned higher or lower on some scale or other, instead of recognizing the mystic uniqueness of each human being. Ways of learning can be evaluated, nevertheless. Liberal democracy is a way to minimize violence in our relations. It is a philosophical affirmation that interests can be reconciled. This is demonstrated by the experience of an infinite number of exchanges.

Liberal democracy is a philosophical refutation of the belief that the interests of flesh-and-blood people can really be antagonistic, that antagonistic conflicts can be resolved only by struggle of the who-beats-whom or the I-kill-you-or-you-kill-me sort. In place of escalation of the struggle, liberal democracy recommends peaceful negotiation. Your killing me is not the only alternative to my killing you. The alternative to war is liberal transaction.

The philosophy of dictatorship applies the laws of the war of people against people to the coexistence of individuals. The philosophy of democracy tries to apply the rules of transaction among individuals to the coexistence of peoples. If I insist that power should derive from transaction, I am a democrat. I have a right to endorse the philosophy of democracy, and no one can prevent me from doing so.

The Philosophy of Democracy

Here's a historiosophical proposition: democracy is the highroad of European history. Using this approach, it is possible to express the history of Europe in broad, inclusive metaphors. Biblical and Athenian democracy were experiments in the reconciliation of fact and value, immanence and transcendence, the real and the desirable. Metaphysical democracy and societal democracy mirror each other. The spiritual and objective-empirical approaches cannot be permanently separated.

The philosophy of history has to be reclaimed from Marxism-Leninism, which has used it badly; the highroad of history led to the gulag and its surviving vestiges. Why not declare that the goal of history is a world order in which there are no concentration camps and never can be any, in which mass murder is not a key industry? The rejection of terror, the rejection of atomic war, democracy within and among all social units, contractual relations according to the rules of the game—it is up to us to declare that this is the meaning and goal of history.

I have a right to say this because it is in my power to say it. Some have claimed that the goal of history was the Third Reich, or the socialist camp, or technical progress, or economic growth. Others have asserted that the philosophy of history is sheer poetry, metaphysics, an arbitrary selection of values, and therefore devoid of scientific merit. I grant them that. But what's wrong with poetry and metaphysics?

We can ask for a world order in which respect for the human being in ourselves and in the other person is the dominant value—a dialectic of autonomy and solidarity. In a democracy, culture means primarily the cultivation of our ties with one another, since for us human beings the most difficult task is to get along with one another, for we instinctively spread out at one another's expense, we are suspicious of one another, we make one another nervous. For that very reason we can regard as a measure of a civilization the degree to which it has succeeded in bringing our social existence under fair and clear-cut rules. We would be at least as justified in agreeing on such a philosophy of history as on tortuous intellectual constructions that boil down to locating the goal of history in some institution or process transcending individual human beings, such as the growing power of a nation-state or the unceasing progress of the economy (who knows toward what).

The philosophy of history is not an "objective truth," but a common agreement. Since we cannot keep from making value judgments on our surroundings, we have a right to take democracy as the best yardstick of value for historical and social change. Experience has demonstrated that every other proposal is less desirable. However many structural difficulties democracy may still have, no one has yet succeeded in devising a more advanced ideology and practice.

Democracy is a delicate balance between freedom and equality, between self-protection and cooperation, between rational selfishness and rational unselfishness. It is the acknowledgment of conflicts and their open discussion, and an agreement to try to resolve conflicts among people. Democracy is the slow, painful effort to put right the blunders that we have incorporated into our conditions of life. It is the age-old and still imperfect practice of the social contract.

As we take our violently self-assertive passions and submit them to the common rules of the game, written and unwritten—deliberating, negotiating, and reaching agreement, lest we kill one another—we refine the culture of democracy. The concept of democracy implies a regulated contention, a moderation of violence, and the art of bringing cooperation out of a multiplicity of contending wills, with a minimum of force and violence.

A democratic system operating within the rules of the game is not a historical necessity; it is the work of human beings, freely chosen, deliberately willed, and artificial, and for that reason it is open and subject to further development. It is creative imagination applied to social conditions. Democracy contains within itself the contradictions and the dialogue of ideal and practice, utopia and experience. The more we regard society as a creation, the more self-evident democracy becomes and the more primitive every form of dictatorship appears.

Although virtually every great philosopher has contributed to its theory, democracy has no single, canonical founding father. Nor are there any guardians qualified ex officio to decide whether an idea is democratic or not. The philosophy of democracy has only been enriched by the arguments of its great adversaries, Hegel and Nietzsche. Everyone knows more or less what democracy is all about, but no one can claim to know it completely by reason of his office.

Real democracy is always limited, to one degree or another. It is a conflict of tradition and utopia, a dream of fulfillment that laughs at reality and a reality that laughs at dreams of fulfillment.

Inherent in European history is a powerful demand for a legal and political order that will guarantee the autonomy of the parts with respect to the whole, and the effective functioning of the whole with respect to the autonomy of the parts. Democratic philosophy seeks to reduce the helplessness of human beings before their own works and before the powers that emerge from their relations, the three great self-devoted alienations called War, State, and Capital, whose priests are at one in looking down sardonically from their elevation on the sacrifices of the individuals struggling at their feet.

Marx was just as great a thinker of democracy as Montesquieu was. The Frenchman was most interested in the relationship of state and society, and Marx, in the relations of capital and labor. Our inventions in both those areas can turn into monsters. Both capital and the state can increase our freedom if we keep them under control, and both can become tyrants if they escape from our control. Both capital and the state have a powerful propensity to get out from under our control.

Political and economic democracy don't go hand in hand; in any given society one may be on the rise while the other is declining. The subject would be of little interest if it were easy to develop democracy in every direction at once, if there were no conflict between the two major tendencies inseparable from democracy—liberalization and equalization, encouraging competition while also helping those who have dropped out of the contest to get back in again. Liberalization and equalization, although they conflict, are meaningless without each other.

Thus democracy, as a transcendent commitment to reconcile the irreconcilable, bears the marks of human creation in all its grotesque grandeur and imperfection. But everything that emerges, if we reject this transcendent value, is incomparably cruder and more miserable.

The Democracy We Have—Among Ourselves

It was no accident that Eastern Europe's most significant democratic movement chose the name Solidarity—a reference to society's spontaneous cohesion, independent of the state, organizing from below, easily driven underground, but ineradicable from the soil.

Our part of the world is looking for its own authentic movement, one that will grow out of the contemporary reality of Central and Eastern Europe. So long as we are unable to reach agreement on who and what we are, we will of necessity imitate others. We are trying to delineate the consciousness of Central Europe, feeling our way, trying to avoid both Eastern and Western models. We could never really approximate the Western ones, even if we wanted to.

The efforts of our Polish friends have now—on the surface—suffered defeat; but the demand for communal self-governance was not a passing tactical gesture, and it will not disappear from the agenda. Where there is no self-government, society falls into a state of passive dependency; it is unable to do anything without directions, and when it gets directions it drags its feet about carrying them out. If there is no self-government, our neglected state economies will stagger to the brink of crisis. The demand for self-government is the organizing focus of the new Central European ideology.

The various communities in solidarity are not so much interested in governmental power as in communication within the broad society and between similarly situated groups. So long as the basis of sovereignty in our countries is not self-government but the "democratic" centralism of the Communist Party, the censorship will maintain the jerry-built structure of power.

Centralized Party rule and censorship are inseparable. Hence the democratic movement is fundamentally anti-censorship. Expanded consumption cannot substitute for freedom of thought, and anyway there's not much chance of getting it; censorship and the shortage economy are also inseparable. Living standards are higher in Hungary than in other communist countries to the same extent that our censorship is milder.

In Central and Eastern Europe, truth-telling is the article in shortest supply. A communication famine stalks the young intelligentsia in particular, but it affects the society as a whole. The Eastern European democratic movement expresses the existing reality and in so doing brings our collective self-portrait to the surface.

We consider intelligent teamwork, not material growth, to be the first of our values. My fed-up countrymen don't need more calories but more human dignity. They need work in which common thinking becomes a creative force. We are anything but collectivists, we don't place the values of the community above the values of individuals. Instead of the community, we speak of circles of friends in which the free and equal relations of autonomous individuals are more valuable than the alleged effectiveness of the organs of power.

In theory it is easier to socialize a communist state than a capitalist society. If the dictatorship relaxes, if there is no fear that the tanks will roll, self-government will spring up of its own accord wherever thinking people work and live together. There is self-government even under a police state, but only in the sphere of private life.

Opinions forced out of the public arena are transferred to the medium of conversation, from the mass media to personal ones. It is this intimate, living verbal tradition that gives our society its original stamp. The assertions and complaints of official propaganda are greeted by the public with instant suspicion, since there can be no legal counterassertions and countercomplaints. Every means of directing opinion is in the hands of the state, yet this gigantic machine, if not altogether powerless, nevertheless has a very limited effect.

Amid this uncontrollable sea of private conversations, our own system of values is beginning to take shape. It is not identical with the state's value system or with that of capitalism. Respect for money and property have not undermined the other values in the moral consciousness of the young intellectuals who set the tone for society's thinking. A kind of undifferentiated good will takes first place for them and makes itself felt more widely than in the circumscribed circle of the bourgeois family organized around consumption.

The network of friends has become very important indeed, and more permanent than the family. Couples come together and break up, but the network remains and lends support to the new couples. People get together to build houses and the like; today I help, tomorrow you help, and the helping hand is never translated into the language of money. A factory brigade may look from the outside like a colorless, inept, bureaucratic outfit, but from the inside, camaraderie, self-defense, and trust in exchanging views are the reality. People here have more friends than people in other countries; friendship is security.

Since the media of communication and the public meeting halls are under the control of the political censorship in Eastern Europe, the network of friends becomes the means of communicating spontaneous public sentiment. The closer you come to the world of the fringe intellectuals, the truer this becomes. The success of this independent ferment cannot be measured by the replacement of one government by another, but by the fact that under the same government society is growing stronger, independent people are multiplying, and the network of conversations uncontrollable from above is becoming denser. Let the government stay on top, we will live our own lives underneath it.

When our lives are bleak and we place our hopes in a change of government, we put our own tasks in the hands of a paternal authority; we delude ourselves, accepting the mythology of deputizing others to do our work for us. Why should we hope for more from a different Party secretary or a different prime minister than from our friends and relations? I have never met a first secretary or a prime minister; I get along without them. I can find more interesting people among my friends.

If we didn't know what state socialism was like, we could still have hopes for it. As it is, we have no illusions about either capitalism or existing socialism. We cannot expect much good from politicians and political systems. The newspapers puff the chroniclers of the political class and cultivate in their readers the mythology of letting the state do it for them. The newspaper, whose lead story tells of some politician leaving on a trip or issuing a statement, is an accomplice in this self-trivialization of the reader; it is an instrument of the political class. The political discourse of the mass media raises up paternal idols before us and attributes profundity to the vacuities of power.

Autonomy's slow revolution does not culminate in new people sitting down in the paneled offices of authority. I cultivate in myself the illusion that the people who are working for autonomy in Eastern Europe have no desire to lounge in the velvet chairs of ministers, in front of microphones and cameras. I could be wrong: people are capable of strange reactions when an opportunity presents itself. Anyway I still say, let those remain in the government who have a weakness for power. My hope is that, since the dictatorship has already lost its revolutionary sheen, governments in Eastern Europe will learn to wield power more graciously.

The most gifted people should be seers, not government officials. For that, they don't need bodyguards, secretaries, and everything else that fills government leaders with a fatuous sense of their own importance. The best minds can only avoid the obligation of corporate self-censorship if they are not obliged to decide for other people and if their material circumstances are ordinary.

Wisdom is a good in itself. Its very existence is its own reward, and it cannot be ranged underneath any higher value. Usefulness, the good of the community, and other such pomposities only obscure the truth. For a radical outlook, power is not a stage but a prison. Institutional honors only harm a thinker; they prompt him to utter formulas. Lofty rank means castration of the brain.

The kind of master from whom I would like to learn would not want to convince me but to help me find my own truth. He would be neither a monk nor a government spokesman, and he would not insist on being right. If he understood something, he might call it to the attention of others as casually as one sits in a chair. He would not ponder over what might be done, but would quietly wait for inspiration to come and tell him what had to be done.

We seek freedom mainly in the areas where we are already freer and can hope to be even more so—where we are our own bosses because we have no superiors, and where we are left most to our own devices: in the area of our free time. The eight hours that we spend at the workplace are not entirely our own. There, if we are lucky and clever, we can do something that we enjoy and that we ourselves consider worthwhile, but there is no guarantee of that; it doesn't depend on us alone. At work we have in effect sold ourselves; we are not our own men and women, but the employer's. Anyone who defines himself by the eight hours he spends earning his bread has given a profound inner affirmation of his dependence. A description of the institutions of the world of work is an extremely impoverished description of a society. Autonomy, if it means anything, means that I am not identical with my status. I sidle away from it. I step into it as into a costume. At work, we are more or less in the realm of compulsion. As it happened, I didn't mind my jobs as a child-welfare worker and an urban sociologist—the two fields where my jobs lasted longest—but I still enjoy most of all sitting down at my desk every morning to work on my manuscripts.

I know many people—machinists, cabinetmakers—who work contentedly in a little shop next to their homes, turning out no more than their collective requires. When I ask them why they work at home, they smile: It's worth more than anything else to work without a boss. Certainly I am freest when writing. It's an added blessing that I also earn a little money now and then from this sinful pastime. I would engage in this written meditation even if I didn't get a penny for it. Free time doesn't mean idle time; it consists of those hours of which we ourselves are the masters. This is our real life, our most precious possession; our free time most resembles ourselves.

The Hungarians have best shown their acumen, perhaps, in their ability to go forward where it was easiest to do so: in the parallel economy and culture—that is, in the sphere of free time. Small businesses, independent seminars, agricultural societies, and *samizdat* publications are organized in private homes. Official premises belong to the state, homes to "society." Home and free time: these are the spatial and temporal dimensions of civic independence.

Seeking the line of least resistance is more a resourceful way of struggling than a timid one. We are not trying primarily to conquer institutions and shape them in our image but to expand the bounds of private existence. People spend their forty-two hours a week working inside formal organizations, but if the remaining one hundred twenty-six are their own, then one cannot help noting—and it is odd that our sociologists have not done so—that considerable scope is available for the development of civil society. The evening and the weekend are yours, you can do with them whatever you wish. At work there is censorship, at home there is none. Just imagine if interesting conversations were going on in a million homes; if someone didn't like it, what could they do about it?

In our society, democratic criticism more often raises objections to the institutional organization of working time, but is that really the most important thing? Those forty-two hours are not the most important part of our human reality, and we even make over some of that time for our own private purposes. Here in Eastern Europe, at least, I don't know anyone who wouldn't try to turn paid working time into private time through a little friendly conversation with a fellow worker, if nothing more. As for the rest, the other one hundred and twenty-six hours, that is a good deal more —even if we are long sleepers, for no one can deny that our dreams are our own. Spreading out our lives before us in the plane of time, we get the surprising and illuminating impression that we spend the greater part of our time, even here in Budapest, in a democracy. The working day is theirs, the free time is ours. If it passes drearily, that's our own fault, because we are dreary. Circumstances cannot be blamed for everything.

Withdrawal into our huddled private circles enabled us to survive even the grimmest years of the dictatorship. We didn't really live in a state of constant tension because every evening we could be with one another. We talked a great deal; congregating in our lairs, we experienced a kind of campfire warmth.

During the Stalin era, to be sure, each citizen was bound over hand and foot to the state. The authorities were not satisfied if he was under their thumb at work alone, or at the university. The great iron hand closed its fingers round our hearts. Many trembled even in their beds, and quite properly, too. Anyone who didn't want to be an enemy of the state was right to tremble just in case he still might look like one (and so become one) anyway.

On Sunday morning the agitator would ring the doorbell: "We are people's educators, here for a little talk; we hope we're not disturbing you." "Oh, not at all, we're very glad to see you." Early Sunday morning we would set out on an excursion so they wouldn't find us at home; or we would listen on all fours by the front door, or sit stock still in our chairs, refusing to answer the door, but fearful afterward that the neighbor, who knew we were home, would report us. That was a black mark, too, and we were certain that somewhere they were keeping track of our black marks.

Parents were not just afraid of outsiders observing them; they were afraid of their own children. "What if he reports what he hears at home, or just stupidly blurts it out?" The state required our free time for "social labor," for communist Sundays, for seminars, meetings, patriotic celebrations, parades, rehearsals for parades, cross-country races, street dances, community sings, collective hikes, and communal newspaper reading hours—anything rather than let us out of their sight and leave us to ourselves! Organized communal life was correct and socialist. Unorganized private life was incorrect and petty bourgeois. The solitary rambler, alone with his dreams, could be an enemy.

Yet it proved impossible to swallow up the citizen body and soul. Man and wife still strolled at length, emptying their hearts to each other. Workmates leaned close in the taverns, illegal parties whispered in the cafés. What we didn't do from sheer mischief, so things wouldn't be the way they were supposed to be, so what was forbidden would happen anyway! An air of sweet deceit bound the whole city together.

Women appeared in the workplace, and somehow that world of strict discipline became less strict. How much serious dedication there was in the girls who belonged to the communist youth movement! Yet their well-steeled souls became soft and sweet in the middle of a kiss. We slipped away from parades slyly and eagerly; we confessed to each other in forest clearings that we were not yet sufficiently hardened atheists; we held hands beside the Danube and gazed at the eternal stars.

The trains that carried the workers were filled not only with exhausted state proletarians but also with young bodies hungry for love and less fearful than before of the priest and the gossip. Instead of going to Marxism-Leninism class you could accompany your sweetheart to the beauty parlor and make fun of the pimply "Party nuns"; you could slip out of the university ball, where Soviet dance music was playing, and go across to the Pipacs Bar, where the pianist played bebop numbers and the drummer sang in English.

From factory gates and office portals, crowds of strollers pour out into the jungle of free time. At home, on the street, in the espresso bars, they meet whomever they wish. The authorities don't prescribe how we should look at each other; our style is our own. The censorship doesn't control what I say to my mother or my son, to my love or my friend. Naturally they are the most important for me, those dearest to me by blood or by choice.

Stranger, pay attention to the liveliness of the conversations in our public squares and at our private parties. If you understand our language, listen to the elderly men and women in the cafés—you'll hear them because they speak loudly. Can you sense that this is literature, too? Hungarians roaming the world often feel homesick for those conversations: the speakers were important to one another— the warmth of the altercations and accusations is proof enough of that. Meaningful exchange takes place at other times, too, as when a hotel clerk puts unrelated travelers into the same room because of lack of space, or when people engage in conversation on a rail journey without even knowing each other's names.

Working time is certainly more intensive in the West,

but free time, I suspect, is every bit as full in Eastern Europe. I seldom encounter here the complaint that people have nothing in common with one another and are unable to converse in a heartfelt way. In Budapest, I believe, loneliness strikes less often than in the great cities of the West. Anyone who wants to can immerse himself in an unbounded sea of talk. I may have less money and fewer rights than if I lived in the West, but I probably have more friends and more free time.

Among whom do ideas circulate with the greatest velocity? Who are the most avid consumers of thought? What do people pass on most eagerly? Who are the most eager readers of uncensored publications? The young intellectuals, of course—the book people, who live and breathe reading and writing, who derive as much enjoyment from the fine arc of an idea as a soccer fan does from a fine free kick. Thinking freely means the most to those who themselves work at the trade of trying to express ideas; they are by vocation the ringleaders in the effort to get round or break through both internal and external censorship.

For whom do I write? For everyone who basically understands what I'm thinking because their minds have been running along the same lines, and because they use their minds rather than allow themselves to become besotted or let themselves run to fat. If there is a thirst for ideas anywhere, it is among the young intellectuals; their reading experiences are the most memorable.

It is a fact that intellectuals write primarily for one another. What's there to be ashamed of in that? My best readers have always been writers. Other people, I notice, also take an interest in what we writers say to one another. I write for myself, for my friends, and for a generalized other person whose age, sex, income, or education I don't know. I imagine someone who is smarter than I am; it's for that person that I write.

What a quixotic ambition it would be for me to aim specially for readers among young workers or middle-aged female officials! I don't pick my readers; my texts are for all those who like to linger over them. I know from experience that my readers are more likely to be university students than retired laborers. Who is it that most requires a consistently thought-out view of the world? Those who are like me.

I find it unobjectionable that I think along the same lines as the hundred thousand young intellectuals who will be setting the tone of opinion as the next millennium approaches. In our schools they are the best students; they are the ones who go on for university degrees, who give the most time to books. Why should I try to make myself understood by those who are poor students and don't like to read? My natural vocation is to contribute to the meditations of my peers.

George Konrád

The Worldwide Integration of the Intelligentsia

Of the social changes that have taken place in the twentieth century and especially since World War II, one of the most interesting has been the emergence of an international network of intellectuals; today we can even speak of an international intelligentsia. The global flow of information proceeds on many different technical and institutional levels, but on all levels the intellectuals are the ones who know most about one another across the frontiers, who keep in touch with one another, and who feel that they are one another's allies.

It was Goethe who first pointed out the existence of a world literature, greater than the sum of national literatures, and since his time that notion has grown ever more meaningful. In the nineteenth century it still meant only European literature, in particular Western European literature. Today, however, we see the development of a worldwide network of ties joining people of every culture and country who have more in common with one another than with the bulk of their countrymen, people who are drawn together by a knowledge of one another's work, even when they haven't met personally.

If a writer or a physicist is imprisoned somewhere, it is an offense to the international solidarity of writers and physicists, and it is especially painful if they know the victim's work. That is the most important thing—the personal network of sympathy, the trade's international circle of friends. This is a form of integration, too, like the nation-state, although it differs radically from it.

We may describe as transnational those intellectuals who are at home in the cultures of other peoples as well as their own. They are wanderers who feel the whole earth is their own. They keep track of what is happening in various places. They have special ties to those countries where they have lived, they have friends all over the world, they hop across the sea to discuss something with their colleagues; they fly to visit one another as easily as their counterparts two hundred years ago rode over to the next town to exchange ideas.

National culture, with its network of schools, universities, academies, theaters, and museums, grew up in the nineteenth century. A global culture with its own institutions is growing up today. National culture represented universality in the face of the parochialism of the various regional units, just as the common national language represented universality in the face of local dialects. Today it is international integration that determines universality, while national culture has an air of provincialism. Individuals, universities, and groups of intellectuals maintain ties across the frontiers today, all over the world, with the cooperation of the nation-state's cultural authorities or without it.

National economies now have to learn the surprising and still scarcely discernible laws of the world market, from which even the strongest economies are not exempt. The world market grows more powerful every day; it is an ever more immediate reality for individual enterprises and their leaders. At the same time a global culture is constantly growing; it is a more palpable and more striking reality every day.

The individual, whether a transmitter of messages or a receiver, can no longer live within a purely national context even if he wants to. Globalization has gone farthest in the natural sciences: today a national physics would be a surrealistic notion. The most advanced disciplines are those which are the most international. The nation is a transitional stage of integration; in the nineteenth century it was wide and spacious, but today it is narrow. Today an international network of intellectual institutions is being formed, independent of governments.

In the leading fields of science, ties extend in every direction, bounding over national frontiers. The global conversation of genius has become the great stimulus to scientific achievement. If one discipline takes a leap forward somewhere, it immediately attracts international interest; other researchers gather round at the news of a striking discovery. Truth has no nationality. Scientists exchange views and places; they learn the special flavor of international friendship, the fascination of thinking along the same lines as someone who lives on the other side of the earth. Today it is the dualism of national and global culture, not that of country and city, that provides the most productive conflict.

The East-West military confrontation saps the vitality of this international market of ideas. Ideological war only strengthens the tensions and suspicions that make us want to belittle what is unknown and foreign rather than get to know it. These tensions are part of the pathos of the national intellectuals and of the role they play.

Not everyone has something worth hearing to say to other nations; it's not easy to be an international intellectual. Many people's thoughts are such that their neighbors, and even their spouses, have little curiosity about them. A global intellectual is someone whose work his peers, at least, all over the world want to know.

The components of world culture are individual works, not national cultures. Any creator whose sights are set on a place in the national pantheon, and who restricts himself to the national rules of decorum in order to enter it, will probably never set foot there and will certainly leave no mark on the international scene.

We now accept as natural that sports achievements, scientific and technical discoveries, and even musical compositions and films are taken notice of and judged on an international scale. Little by little, the same thing is happening in every intellectual discipline. Today all artists are engaged in individual world class competition. It is a competition in which all the members of a national galaxy shine more brightly by one another's light, and yet each one of them can enter the contest only on an individual basis.

The existence of a world forum favors the emergence of the eccentric, of those who stand out. From afar, it is not the good boys who attract interest, but those rare and extraordinary beings whose like is not found near at hand. The intellectual alliance of dissenters and avant-gardists takes under its wing those few people who, in their various ways, think their thoughts through to the end.

Every culture has its own diaspora, and the Eastern European cultures have them to a marked degree. Those who couldn't square their mental logic with conditions at home have scattered to the four winds, and they have often found a more congenial medium for their efforts abroad. Wanderers in search of knowledge want to learn more than can be learned in their national cultures. In emigration, many are freed from the penalties and discriminatory pressures that greeted their individuality at home. On the world market, every work remains available for as long as its quality merits it. The most assiduous national patronage cannot lift a mediocre work onto the saucy and democratic stage of world culture and keep it there.

Fortunately, we don't depend on our own governments alone. If we did, we might have to be put into a straitjacket from time to time. The trip abroad, the forming of friendships with others across the frontier—these are some of the elements of the intellectuals' struggle for freedom; the international Solidarity of the craft is their mutual defense alliance.

It appears that the intelligentsia—not the working class—is the special bearer of internationalism. It is obvious that those who study for twenty years are better attuned to the wider world than those who go to school for only eight. The intellectuals have worked out a whole infrastructure of international communication. Theirs is a network of institutions no less dynamic and developing than that of the nation-state. Never have intellectuals flitted so readily from one continent to another; no one gets around as much as they do, whether as stars, members of the global elite of their fields, or simply as ordinary knights errant of the spirit.

They have friends in every corner of the globe, something that cannot be said of the workers. The working class is more national than the intelligentsia. It seemed that the intellectuals were a more national class only so long as the nation-state formed their mental horizon (just as the factory formed that of the worker and the village that of the peasant). Even then the intellectuals stood one step higher in terms of the range of their outlook. Today everyone has moved up a step in terms of the breadth of their purview and identification.

The same person may play both a national and an international role. Even the most ardent patriots hate to be left out of the intelligentsia's ritual of international contacts, the opportunities to take the stage at symposia, seminars, conferences, and congresses, for everyone likes to travel, especially if some institution is picking up the tab.

A whole host of value judgments revolve around the poles of this dialectic of the national and the international. No one is purely national or purely international. Any suppression of one role for the sake of the other produces singular spiritual blossoms; the way we deal with this duality in ourselves is itself a rich theme for meditation. In the next century it will no longer be so, perhaps; even today this duality is a more settled, less emotional issue in Western than in Eastern Europe. We live in more closed national cultures here, for the nation-state casts its shadow over us all.

This problem has passionately engaged my friends and acquaintances at various times in their lives. It goes hand in hand with the dilemma of whether to stay or emigrate—a problem whose emotional charge is evidenced by the emigration of some ten thousand Hungarians every year. This is a question heavy with moral dramas, philosophical strategies, and anxious soul-searching. To step across the border to the West is to step out of our state culture. It means that for a time we don't need to be afraid of the things we ordinarily fear. In the colors and artifacts, in the faces and bearing of the people, we see a greater richness and variety of freedom. It takes a little patriotic determination to welcome once again the coziness of our less variegated existence, rather than just dragging ourselves home resignedly when our travel permits expire, like furloughed soldiers returning to barracks.

National culture, which of course has roots in a certain environment, turns into a distinct nation-state culture when it comes under state supervision and becomes amenable to state control—when, in other words, it comes to bear the marks of censorship, both external and internal. Nation-state culture is a narrower concept than national culture; it tends to exclude the Hungarians living in other countries and those living in inner emigration at home, along with their works, and it excludes them all the more sharply, the more mistrustful and insincere our political life is.

Where there is no democracy, a permit is required to take manuscripts abroad, and any writer who sends his work abroad without one is a smuggler. The same is true even of the gentle reader who carries "forbidden" literature across the frontier. The customs authorities have a strict obligation to prevent the influx of books that have been put on the index. Politically reliable or merely timid authors will not submit for publication or translation any works for which their more politically reliable superiors might later condemn them. In a closed culture minds work overtime; even those who think they are in opposition are full of the critical prejudices of the powerful.

The most effective antidote to state monopoly, in culture as in other areas, is the world market. The reliable, censored cultural product, laden with state prizes though it be, finds few takers on the world culture market. Dissident culture, on the other hand, does get into circulation, which the censor mentality explains by charging that the enemy supports it. Since what is antistate must at the same time be worthless, dissident culture cannot have any value.

The state may be hostile toward the international network, but it cannot be victorious over it. The public of the wider world makes the final judgment. It is unlikely that the Cannes Film Festival or the Frankfurt Book Fair will make judgments of value inferior to those of state culture's high command. "Hard goods" on the world market become a kind of international cultural reality, independent of the national reality and indeed superseding it. An international public opinion reflecting the influence of international culture can become a counterweight to the state's cultural dictatorship; it can curb the tendency of the sovereign state to become omnicompetent.

In the eyes of world opinion, national prejudices are only a curiosity. Local praise makes the same impression as a state travel agency brochure. The foreign reader can hardly be blamed for preferring something which in his country is unusually honest and outspoken, or the likes of which he cannot find at home. He can get enough respectful commonplaces in his own country, probably in more sophisticated form, so why bother to import more of the same, and in cruder form?

The dissidents' international market of ideas has taken its place alongside the international news and weather services. We have come to expect that Latin American dissidents— rather than the protégés of the military dictatorships—will find publishers in Europe. Is it any wonder if the same thing is true of Eastern Europe?

THE POWER OF THE STATE AND THE POWER OF THE SPIRIT: POLITICS AND ANTIPOLITICS

Today the intellectuals' product is the leading product; knowledge is the prime commodity in trade. High-grade skills, life styles, new options will be the competitive items of the turn of the millennium. The royal road is the road of software. Creative imagination is the thing that costs the most. What exists is what we think up—as it always has been, sometimes with a vengeance. Marx, Einstein, Freud: you bet people pay attention when someone has one or two intriguing ideas! Indeed, they parrot them ad nauseam, riding even the most original ideas to the point of inanity.

Those who have the greatest stake in the global information market are the international intellectual elite, who are no longer content to remain within the national arena. It is the difference between circling the globe (several times) and strolling over to visit your next-door neighbor. I am a futurist from the depths of our history. We no longer need to offer our services to hard-riding noblemen, mustachioed hussars, potbellied capitalists, leather-coated revolutionaries, and somber-suited ministers; gone is our inferiority toward these caricatures. We are in a relatively secure position: they can't get along without us.

Everyone tries to make what he has marketable. We have an interest in seeing that intellectual ability is valued most highly. This is the global conspiracy of the international intellectual elite—the first conspiracy in history that doesn't need to be kept secret. It is a conspiracy against the global coalition of aggressive imbecility. Let no one deceive us into thinking that the aggressive imbeciles mouth their vicious inanities against each other. They are allies; two dictators making war on each other are hand in glove to the extent that they jointly call attention to themselves and use the other's existence as an excuse to silence opposition at home.

It's a competition for minds, for followers, for disciples, for the public. It's a prophets' market: how many copies can you sell your inspiration in? Alluring ideas, ideas that elevate and wound, ideas whose marketability is partly in the pain they cause—a full supply of ways of thinking on the international market of ideas, competition of styles on the international market of styles! It's a game every bit as eventful as the Olympics or the arms race. For it isn't just news that travels along the global networks, it's new ideas as well. Not only can we find out in one corner of the world what's happening in another corner, we can find out what people there are thinking about, too. The worldwide connections of the media have put an end to closed cultures with incommensurable values of no use to others.

Our societies are systems, but nonexclusive systems constantly impinging on one another; some intellectuals play the part of merchants and smugglers, others the role of customs officers. The thinking ones are frontier violators, the censors are the border guards. Our intellectual weight is in direct proportion to the number of border violations we commit.

The cerebrum is liberating itself. The imagination is taking off its clerical-military uniform. The writer isn't a mayor or a Nietzschean blond beast or a professional revolutionary; he isn't a Grand Inquisitor for the state or an expert adviser available for hire to some political leader. Independent thinking doesn't serve the bureaucracy or the bourgeoisie or the proletariat; it serves itself, serves the cause of independent thinking. It identifies rebelliously with itself and refuses to undertake any social obligations to anything alien to itself.

Yesterday's intellectual elites were ashamed of having nothing to offer for sale but the adventure of the understanding and the imagination, devoid of anything more of utility. They wanted some stronger justification for their existence, some nobler warrant for their income and social position. The consciousness of the intellectuals wasn't enough for them. They longed for a more exciting role, for noble, heroic, military qualities.

The adepts of thinking felt a snobbish awe for the Deed—

which in the last analysis usually means some violent act: war, revolution, the forcible expansion of a nation or a class. For killing, in other words, or what is almost the same thing —giving license to kill. Intellectuals who turned their backs on intellectual power and embraced physical force felt smugly superior toward niggling humanists. Things generally ended, of course, with these hysterical militants being first used, then patronized, and then, once they had served their purpose, being elbowed aside by the bureaucrats, politicians, and soldiers.

The intelligentsia is responsible for its own bad conscience. It has itself brought the intellect into disrepute. Professing faith in the primacy of instinct, feeling, and material interest is self-torture for the intellectual. It is the pseudoethical mask of the dependent intellectual, the employee, the servant. Priests have been replaced by men of the state. A revolutionary of the Left or Right is a state man, too—at least he will be if he wins. He will consent to having his most valuable possession expropriated—his ability to think.

A dictatorship may have good technology, but it will never have a good literature, except in opposition. (True, where the language of symbols languishes, technical thinking will eventually languish, too.) Existing authority and independent reflection look at each other with suspicion— the executive and the creator, the censor and the artist.

The power of the spirit and the power of the state are irreconcilable. Theirs is a deadly serious struggle: which will take over the other from within? This is a combat that requires not one drop of blood nor any great commotion, only a clear and constant awareness that here two radically different powers are at work.

We have no reason at all to think that the age-old separation of spiritual and worldly power is an anachronism. Combining the two in the unitary power and culture of the socialist state was a misguided utopia. There would be no democracy today if the Catholic Church had not been an independent power with respect to armed secular authority. Marxism-Leninism's unitary state culture is a Russian development, a continuation of the tradition that made the czar head of the church as well as of the state. Where there is no separate spiritual authority, culture is subservient and false.

How crude a theoretical construction state Marxism is can be seen even from the fact that it bears the name of no single person (for which the genius of Marx can hardly be blamed). Marxism was Lenin's work, as Marxism-Leninism was Stalin's. Anyone who calls himself a Marxist-Leninist is in fact a Stalinist. It is Stalin who deserves the credit for formulating Marxism-Leninism into a closed and sharply distinct state ideology. An open, creative Marxism-Leninism doesn't exist. Without the guarantee of the Soviet-type party state, the doctrine falls apart. Eliminate the Stalinism from Marxism-Leninism and you eliminate the essence— the fact that this ideology is an educational system, centrally directed under Moscow's auspices, for the Soviet state and its dependencies.

It was Stalin's achievement to fuse state and doctrine into a single, closed entity; neither can exist without the other. The theoretical fiction of the universal and incontrovertible validity of Marxist-Leninist doctrine, and its rigid definition and institutionalization, were essential to the campaign to stamp out "diversionists, spies, wreckers, and assassins" who hid with diabolical cunning behind the mask of ideological deviation. The gulag waited for deviationists.

It is obligatory in the Communist countries to study Marxist-Leninist science; it is forbidden, or at least inadvisable, to question it. For Marxism-Leninism to come into existence at all, and to acquire the authority to command and forbid, many millions of innocent people had to die. Without the police state, the crude and arbitrary propositions of this orthodoxy would collapse into an incoherent heap. If Marx the thinker is to become our contemporary in all the original freshness of his thought, it can only be by clearing away the encrustations of Marxism-Leninism—the ideology of the Russian police state, great Stalin's work.

The favorites of the great feudal lords of yesterday wanted to become feudal lords themselves; they were not content with the power of ideas. They craved the prestige of office and the power to command. They went into state service in order to be somebody. They thought they had to put on a costume and adopt an elevated manner so that people would listen to them.

To worry is human, and it is understandable that mediocrities should worry; they require the exaltation of service. The radical intelligence exists for its own sake; it is no essential part of its purpose that anyone should find any use for it. At most, it is useful in the same way as the urinal that Marcel Duchamp once exhibited—to be contemplated rather than employed.

In its essential operations, knowledge is identical with itself, and that's enough for it. Our powers are finite, the next sentence completely engages our attention; our minds don't go on to wonder what others may say about it. The others come in only when they read our pages, are entertained by them, or push them aside—that is their business. It is a pleasant though sometimes disquieting surprise when someone makes use of our ideas. How many people can use our texts? We will find out on the market.

Can't you just smell the odor of the musty moralists whom these words will stir up? Virtuous lackeys, prominent public personalities, the whores of power will all come running to call us to order and unctuously preach a little respect. They will say that service is the road to greatness. Refusing ideological service is blatant self-absorption, narcissism. The statesman, they will say, dutifully looks after his fellow man. Yes, indeed—just as the jailer does.

Spiritual authority differs from political authority in that it only grows stronger from opposition and controversy. It's a good thing if an original idea produces heated opposition at first. A creative intellectual who doesn't provoke irritation and even hatred is perhaps not so creative as he thinks. If the time comes when everyone loves and respects him, he is finished.

The reality of spiritual power is a conversation of a few minds, smiling conspiratorially at one another across frontiers and oceans. To serve others, they need no church and no platform. They don't need to dress up in costume so others will listen to them. They don't pretend that they're on top for the sake of others.

What does it mean, anyway, to say that an intellectual is "on top"? It means no one is giving him orders. It means he is free. An intellectual has spiritual authority only if he refuses to censor himself for the sake of the state, the public, or the good Lord himself. An intellectual who is on top is one who shows his own face—every aspect of it.

Armed authority is not to be trifled with; spiritual authority, on the other hand, asks to be played with. It doesn't want to hear its obituary read in its own lifetime. The creative intellectual is ill at ease in the mask of any ideology. He is on top if he refuses to sell his brains to any interest independent of himself—if, instead of making what they order from him, he gets them to buy what he has made.

The creative intellectual will be on top when there is no longer any institution—state, church, industrial enterprise, university—that can use him as an instrument. He will not rest until he can contract on an equal footing with them, until a value system comes into being that will esteem greater knowledge and ability. In reality, spiritual authority is a state of mind; it is—to give it old-fashioned names—inspiration, illumination.

Without disputing the Church's title to the name, it still seems to me that a really catholic universalism—one that holds all particularisms in check—is represented most authentically today by the international intellectual aristocracy. Today it is not enough to pray for peace; today one must think for peace—not piously, but radically.

At a time when the representatives of the nation-state discourse solemnly on the theoretical possibility of mass

annihilation; when the leaders of the superpowers themselves cannot clearly say if they want to win or to settle,
when intellectual luminaries in goodly numbers advance
general principles to justify a patriotic particularism armed
for victory—at such a time one must declare that the interests of one country are not the supreme value, that our
country is not what is most important.

What I have in mind is not some kind of anarchic, romantic rising; the time for that sort of thing is long past.
The movement for intellectual autonomy need not bring
great masses of people out into the streets. There is no need
to incite young people to shower stones on the police. The
important questions will not be decided amid the scufflings
of demonstrators and police; street theater is a rather super-
ficial symbol.

For intellectual autonomy, it is not necessary to start a
general strike against the government under the banner of
simplistic slogans. The most effective way to influence
policy is by changing a society's customary thinking patterns
and tacit compacts, by bringing the pace-setters to think
differently. No, I am not thinking of neurotic defiance of all
authority. On the contrary, I am thinking of the authority
of the spirit.

The intellectual aristocracy has no desire to bring down
governments, since its members don't want to be government leaders. They are aristocratic in nature precisely because they do and will go on doing what they like to do, and
for that reason they are perhaps happier than government
officials. The political, economic, military, and cultural
bureaucracies need not fear the intellectual aristocrats, since
the latter don't envy any of them. Any intellectuals who

choose to compete for central-government advisory or executive posts are already doubtful members of the intellectual aristocracy.

The intellectual aristocracy is content to push the state administration in the direction of more intelligent, more responsible strategies. Its members do this as a part of the self-governing intellectual community, even though they act individually, independent of the state. This is the spiritual authority that the most significant writers, thinkers, scholars, and artists have exercised for thousands of years.

Karl Marx is not there behind the Party secretary, even though his picture hangs on the wall behind him while the Party secretary talks stuff that would enrage Marx or put him to sleep. Marx is here beside us, and in the midst of all those who have heads on their shoulders and dare to use them. The intellectual aristocrats have pledged themselves to an indivisible world culture, in the teeth of every contemporary institution and every forum of authority. They are loyal to Montaigne and Spinoza, Goethe and Tolstoy, but not by any stretch of the imagination to a mere head of state or Party secretary. Ever since Tolstoy, it has been a simple rule of literary decorum to display at least as much independence toward the leaders of the state as he displayed toward the czar.

This authority, with its purely intellectual operations, reduces to its proper place in the public's eyes the authority of states, parties, armies, industries—of every organized institution, in short—and in its place elevates that of Plato, the Bible, and the Tao. A little open aristocratism is necessary lest the great democrats run off with democracy.

The more imaginative are better able to envisage human suffering than those who cause it—those people who display an astonishingly abstract insensitivity toward concrete human pain, whose powers of empathy are often surprisingly scanty (as the rhetorical hollowness of the language most of them use so clearly reveals), who are capable of imagining a relatively favorable nuclear exchange (otherwise why would they be planning for it?).

The autonomy of the intellectuals has outgrown this adolescent game of soldiers. They are no longer enchanted by the equally adolescent knightly virtues of a noble-chivalric culture. The patriotic cobbler can stay in the old rotogravure album, along with the even more patriotic students who spiked a bayonet for country, for king, for Hitler, for Stalin, hurrah! We are no longer susceptible to the romance of the professional revolutionary, the suicide squad, the terrorist, or the secret police conspiracy; behind the mask of militancy the face of the immature adult is all too evident.

It is my impression that today, at the end of the second millennium, we have to be adults; otherwise there's going to be trouble. This time it is not a matter of noble adolescents rebelling against wicked adults. The last rationalized adolescent rebellion, that of the 1960s, has been weighed and found wanting. I don't see in youth culture an alternative to the prevailing claustrophobia. The open meditation of mature men and women is needed. It won't bother me if the adolescents aren't interested. The time is coming, quietly but perceptibly, for the learners to start teaching, as soon as they are ready.

———

A society does not become politically conscious when it shares some political philosophy, but rather when it refuses to be fooled by any of them. The apolitical person is only the dupe of the professional politician, whose real adversary is the antipolitician. It is the antipolitician who wants to keep the scope of government policy (especially that of its military apparatus) under the control of civil society.

The antipolitician is not a representative of spiritual authority, but rather its repository: his person and function are indivisible. The politicians and their intellectual employees pollute the intellectual environment in the hope that the population whom they target through the media will be unable to think in any terms other than the ones they present.

Their product is the cheerleader, the political dupe; the good party member (of any party); the loyal and unknown soldier who leaves the decisions to his superior while he charges to his death; the young people who can always be brought out for parades; the technicians of oppression who willingly commit atrocities because, if they have orders from above to do it, it cannot be an atrocity. Their product is the stultification of the average person. In fact, it is not difficult to bring even lucid minds to this deplorable state; one need only start careful ideological education while they are still young, in early childhood if possible.

In the West, ambitious people aim, in their business or political careers, for the very top. Everything goes toward success, and the ne plus ultra of success is to be number one—to win the title of managing director or President of the Republic. To become President tops off a supercareer.

And the losers shouldn't be ashamed; after all, it was fair play, they elected him, he's their temporary king. For a few years he can beam with satisfaction. For a few years people will admire his picture; he is interchangeable with them. They can praise him or berate him, he's still the one—he and his aides and a few others who, in the struggles round the throne, aspire to succeed him. The newspapers speak of Roosevelt's America, Churchill's England, de Gaulle's France, Adenauer's Germany (to mention only the dead), and with good reason, just as the historians speak of Napoleonic France, Victorian England, or Wilhelmine Germany. The country is the ruler's, whether crowned or elevated by electoral majority.

We Eastern Europeans, however, have been ruled so long and so shamelessly by kings, generals, admirals, and Party secretaries, good and bad, that the question of who rides in the first carriage of state interests us less than the question: how well do we sleep in our beds? How much are we at the mercy of a whole pyramid of bosses, topped by the president–Party secretary–king (who may at the same time be generalissimo and police chief as well)?

What occupies our minds above all in Eastern Europe is not whether a policy is good or bad, but the overabundance of policies everywhere. The state drags countless matters, questions, and decisions into politics that have no business there—private matters or technical questions with which, in the last analysis, the state has nothing to do.

The question of how this text will reach the Hungarian or perhaps foreign reader, for example, would never engage the attention of a Western democracy. That is a matter— normally—for me and my publisher alone to decide. It doesn't concern the minister of culture, the Party central committee, the police, the customs service, and the many other organs whose meddling the Hungarian taxpayers support. How much trouble it must be to watch the printers, to make sure they don't print it (assuming they don't simply lock up the author on one charge or another). This example shows as clearly as any how a purely private matter becomes, under state socialism, a preeminently political matter. There are far more pressing tasks for my fellow citizens than trying to prevent my meditations from reaching potential readers. So I don't ask for a different policy toward my writings; I ask for no policy at all. Every reader can substitute his own private affairs in place of my writings. I don't want different cultural policies, I want fewer cultural policies and cultural politicians.

Because politics has flooded nearly every nook and cranny of our lives, I would like to see the flood recede. We ought to depoliticize our lives, free them from politics as from some contagious infection. We ought to free our simple everyday affairs from considerations of politics. I ask that the state do what it's supposed to do, and do it well. But it should not do things that are society's business, not the state's. So I would describe the democratic opposition as not a political but an antipolitical opposition, since its essential activity is to work for destatification.

The antipoliticians—and in secret there are many of them —want to free biology and religion, rock music and animal husbandry from the pathological bloat of the political state. Wherever the number of informers, provocateurs, and police agents per thousand inhabitants is higher than it is in, say, Iceland, then it's time for the state to slim down. An antipolitician is someone who wants to put the state on a strict diet and doesn't mind being called antistate because of it.

The question is: more state or less? Those who want more state, stand over here; those who want less, over there. Possibly we have reached the point where even those who would like less will say they want more, because they don't trust their own minds any longer. They are state men, they have state minds; in their dreams the state rings the doorbell and takes them away. Yesterday's terror has become tonight's bad dream. We must push the state out of our nightmares, so as to be afraid of it less. That is antipolitics.

Socializing state socialism will be a task for one or two antipolitical generations—not apolitical ones, which act as if all this doesn't concern them. Those who call themselves apolitical are either mistaken or not telling the truth. In fact they are very political indeed; they conduct their entire lives in such a way as to avoid running up against politics. Thus they are constantly influenced by politics—withdrawn, hunkered down in their mouseholes, hiding from the tabby of politics. They are very political indeed. The cat will eat them, if that's what it takes to keep order, lest they skitter back and forth, indulging in merry antifeline squeaking. The apolitical ones very much respect the cat and don't let themselves be carried away with ironical squeaking at her expense.

Antipolitics is the political activity of those who don't want to be politicians and who refuse to share in power. Antipolitics is the emergence of independent forums that can be appealed to against political power; it is a counter-power that cannot take power and does not wish to. Power it has already, here and now, by reason of its moral and cultural weight. If a notable scholar or writer takes a ministerial post in a government, he thereby puts his previous work aside. Henceforth he must stand his ground as a representative of his government, and in upholding his actions against the criticisms of democratic antipolitics he may not use his scholarly or literary distinction as either a defense or an excuse.

Antipolitics and government work in two different dimensions, two separate spheres. Antipolitics neither supports nor opposes governments; it is something different. Its people are fine right where they are; they form a network that keeps watch on political power, exerting pressure on the basis of their cultural and moral stature alone, not through any electoral legitimacy. That is their right and their obligation, but above all it is their self-defense. A rich historical tradition helps them exercise their right.

Antipolitics is the rejection of the power monopoly of the political class. The relationship between politics and antipolitics is like the relationship between two mountains: neither one tries to usurp the other's place; neither one can eliminate or replace the other. If the political opposition comes to power, antipolitics keeps at the same distance from, and shows the same independence of, the new government. It will do so even if the new government is made up of sympathetic individuals, friends perhaps; indeed, in such cases it will have the greatest need for independence and distance.

In his thinking, the antipolitician is not politic. He doesn't ask himself whether it is a practical, useful, politic thing to express his opinion openly. In contrast with the secrecy of the leadership, antipolitics means publicity; it is a power exercised directly over society, through civil courage, and one that differs by definition from any present or future power of the state.

Antipolitics means perspicacity; it means ineradicable suspicion toward the mass of political judgments that surround us. Often these judgments are simply aggression in another form. We shouldn't forget that older men whose physical and nervous energies are failing are especially prone to intellectual aggression of the most savage and relentless kind, though always in the name of noble ideals. Spiritual authority is the practice of this kind of antipolitical understanding.

But what does spiritual authority have to offer that is positive? How is it anything more than sheer negativity? It asserts the worth of human life as a value in itself, not requiring further justification. It respects human beings' fear of death. It views the lives of people of other countries and cultures as equal in value to those of our countrymen. It refuses to license killing on any political grounds whatever. I regard the commandment "Thou shalt not kill" as an absolute command. I have never killed, I want to avoid killing, yet it's not impossible that situations may arise in which I will kill. If I do, I will be a murderer and will consider myself one. Murderers must expiate their crimes.

Antipolitics looks kindly on the ecumenical variety of religions and styles and doesn't believe that the condition for the existence of one cultural reality is the extinction of another.

Antipolitics prefers qualitative competition to silly quantitative questions about who is stronger. Who is stronger is really of no interest. For the antipolitician, it is more interesting to know whether a community produces an intelligent and honest portrait of itself, not how much technical power it commands.

Antipolitics asserts the right of every community to defend itself, with adequate defensive weapons, against occupiers. It is a great misfortune to have to fire on occupiers. We would become murderers ourselves in so doing, but it may happen that we will decide we have to be murderers.

The Creative Intelligentsia and Freedom

The emancipation of the intellectuals is no different from the emancipation of the workers: It is the release of human abilities to express themselves more easily and enjoyably. There is no great difference between the sculptor and the machinist or woodworker. A born doctor and a born auto mechanic readily understand each other. Between the biologist and the gardener there is no class contradiction. All these roles are alike in that solitary concentration is the most essential aspect of the work involved. The important thing is not giving orders or directing other people's work, but the painstaking confrontation with the material (which may also be symbolic or emotional). Study and experiment are the essence rather than teaching or direction, although these too are occasionally indispensable.

Even the film director or research supervisor is not distinguished by the power he has but by his vision, which can be realized only through teamwork. The writer has to deal at times with a publishing executive, but it is not his goal to become a publishing executive himself. The writer's goal is to have the publisher issue his book without changes in as many copies as possible, pay him the largest possible royalty for it, and try to sell as many copies as he can.

Creative intellectuals don't want to be bosses; they want to be able to tinker, to invent, to create what they have imagined. Our utopia is quite simple: it is enough to be able to work—something magnificent in itself, provided our labors are not humiliating and useless. The creative intellectual is the superworker, the one who undertakes the most complicated kinds of activity. He is all right if he can offer his abilities on his own terms, not on the buyer's.

No one will rest until the market for culture belongs to proprietors of ability. They will not rest until they get what belongs to them—their spiritual authority, the authority of ability on the market of labor and ideas. That's been true since the beginning, for thousands of years. The liberation of the intellectuals has been going on all that time and will never end.

The least that we want is recognition that we are the shamans. It is not true that a separate peace can be made with the creators. It is not true that they can be herded into the sheepfolds of the universities. It is not true that talent can be shut up in the padded cells of the communist Bedlam.

No deals are possible here. You can slaughter ability, shut it up in mental hospitals, hope that for the time being it's been bought off. But these people cannot rest so long as the jackasses in power go on insisting: if you want to survive, if you want to live, be a jackass, too. When a talent turns meek, then—dear jackasses—look in his eyes: he's laughing at you. He'll put up with it for a bit, then say: "Back to your place, my friend."

The conflict between capital and labor is beginning to concern us less than the one between those who on the one hand, to maintain existing power relations, try to limit others' freedom of work, of discovery and innovation, and of critical thinking, and those who on the other hand want to work tranquilly and well, without hindrance, who work enough on their own and want thus to earn an honest living.

Hardworking people don't crave luxury; that's not on their minds. Their dispositions demand finer and more genuine pleasures. They find it ridiculous that anyone would try to impress others by spending freely. The great scientists and writers have been rather modest people. The scientist and the jack of all trades are alike in that they find enjoyment in discovering things. They like to work until they're thoroughly tired and then sit around in the evening drinking with friends. They differ from all those whose main occupation is to harass others, take them to task, terrorize and confuse them, even on occasion destroy them. So it's those who work versus those who make trouble.

There are people who like to run everything and make decisions about other people. It doesn't matter if they only

indulge their natural proclivities by doing so and inciden-
tally earn a larger income than the rest of us. But they
are bound to arouse our resentment if they insist on making
us do stupid work, or arrogantly prevent us from doing our
best, or loudly pretend they know the job better than we do
when they don't, or pay too little for us to live without
scrimping while they spend measureless sums on private or
public luxuries (including tanks and missiles, the baubles
of the state), or prescribe what we will like and dislike
(mostly not what we would choose to like and dislike ourselves).

The struggle for freedom of work is continual, and of
course it will never end. Our philosophical aberrations im-
pede this struggle and divert it from its course, and they
may create goals for us that actually narrow the dignity and
freedom of work even when we were hoping for the opposite. Communism was one such aberration on the road
toward the liberation of work. Above the world of peaceable
working people it elevated a bumbling fraternity of noisy
order-givers. Today they are not called capitalists—the name
is different. But they are in charge not only on the job but
everywhere else as well—the same people everywhere; their
ears are listening even in the ceiling of my home. If they
were simply businessmen, they would publish what I write.
As it is, they even make it difficult for me to circulate my
novel in a few dozen photocopies, and they squander huge
sums and keep countless able-bodied people busy to do it.

I don't like communism because I see it as a coherent
system of pointless prohibitions and abridgments of freedom. (It doesn't follow from this that I have to like capitalism, in reaction to which communism arose, since the fact

of communist exploitation doesn't put a prettier face on capitalist exploitation.) When the ideas of the most earnest people in a society are known to only a fraction of the others in that society because state culture acts more like a Chinese wall than a medium of communication, then the system of cultural institutions rightly becomes a target of criticism. Uninspired worthies shouldn't take heart from the fact that in the opposing military camp uninspired worthies also get to the top from time to time. There is every reason for them to cringe before the penetrating gaze of the working people, who see right through them.

The professional revolutionaries claimed that they were the vanguard of the working class. Lo and behold, they turned into the ruling elite, the political bureaucracy of the state-socialist dictatorship—provided they didn't fall victim to some purge or, having survived prison, go back to looking at the world with the eyes of ordinary working, thinking, peaceable, power-spurning people.

The professional revolutionaries (later bureaucrats) are the propagators and victims of the illusion that they stand for the masses and thus make the immediate participation of these masses unnecessary. They fill the role of militant authority. They would like us to believe that they are the embodiment of an impersonal dignity more powerful than that of the masses, and that they symbolize the highest and most general authority, whose directions the masses are obliged to carry out willingly. The Party stands in for the working class, as the state apparatus stands in for the population of the country.

There is no social contract without representation, but here the representative himself declares that he rightfully represents us. He has himself elected by the constituents, and if any of them question whether he really represents them, he claps them in jail, declares them insane, or brands them as vicious, selfish, lonely deviants who are certainly isolated cases (surviving at most in tiny groups of like-minded heretics) in relation to the rest of the community, the whole country, the whole society, which would never express a different opinion on the subject from that of its self-appointed representatives, who keep those they represent in line through police measures.

It is my impression that communism overdoes the principle of representation a bit. So long as it permits elections only with a single list of candidates, like those through which Hitler convinced the world he really was the leader of the German people and entitled to act in their name, it will have trouble persuading sensible people that the politburo of the central committee of the Communist Party really represents the will of at least 98 of every 100 countrymen of ours and therefore has the right to decide for us and about us. They don't represent *me*. The censorship that makes impossible the legal publication of this book in Hungary is no wish of mine.

We might also say that the creative intelligentsia is the vanguard of the working class. We certainly might say it with more reason of those whose place in society is marked out by ability, not power, rather than of politicians who set themselves up by right of power, not ability, over the rest of us who have no power, to tell us what to do and not do. However, let's refrain from saying such a thing.

The mathematician and the poet are not what they are

because of something else; they are mathematician and poet in their own right. It is quite impossible to elect or appoint anyone to be a mathematician or a poet. By the same token, it is impossible to relieve anyone of either distinction. They are what they are because ever since childhood they have been playing with mathematical or poetic symbolism, whether they get paid for it or not, whether other people like it or not. It is unnecessary to justify what they do by citing the interests of others. They know with the certainty of faith that these two ancient crafts, mathematics and poetry, are good. If thrown into prison, they will beguile the time with them there as well.

The same cannot really be said of, let's say, a prison warden. Lock him up and he will unquestionably cease to be a prison warden once on the other side of the bars. Let's be content to say that there is probably some connection between an increase of freedom for the creative intelligentsia and an increase of freedom for the workers. But we ought to regard this too as only a hypothesis to be compared with experience; it would have to be tested, to see if it really is so.

The personal doesn't seek to conceal itself in the impersonal. It's not important whether I look like an official or a university teacher, or even a writer, as long as I look like somebody. I speak in my own name, not in the costume of some role or other. I would like to write what comes to my mind, not stagger along under the weight of the petrified ideas of earlier times. Indeed, I live by the fact that I write only in my own name. Further, I have noticed that others too would like to speak in their own names. Many young intellectuals are thinking along the same lines as I am. They would like to let their minds roam freely, with a minimum of pressure and banality. I regard my readers as accomplices in that desire.

The techniques and advances of printing, the simple procedures of private reproduction, facilitate our discourse. Readers and writers ought to learn the techniques of reproduction, just as they learn to use the typewriter. These techniques—newer and simpler ways of propagating words —can increase the circle of kindred spirits tenfold or even a hundredfold, while making the censor's work more difficult. Expanding our technical skills in the art of communicating words is a civic obligation of ours so long as censorship exists.

In cities where there is no censorship, photocopiers are available on every corner, in every bookstore. Residents of Budapest will know they live in a free society when they can go into a photocopying shop and make as many copies of their manuscripts as they can pay for. The number of photocopiers per thousand population is not a bad index of freedom. The day when the newspapers are full of ads for duplicators will be the day when we can start to consider Hungary a civilized country. There is no censorship here, our politicians say. To that, it is enough to remark that the photocopiers in our industrial enterprises are kept under the strict supervision of the ministry of interior.

For centuries, the prejudices of the monastic copyist had to be reckoned with, since the copyist both acted as a medium of diffusion and exercised a form of censorship. After Gutenberg, writers no longer needed to disguise themselves as monks in order to circulate their works. Intellectuals could forget about the demands of piety.

The revolutions of duplication and long-distance tele-communications work in favor of freedom. In our time it seems to be the techniques of information transmission that develop the fastest; technology dissolves the unhealthy exclusiveness of the nation-state.

If I take a map of the world and blacken the countries where there is state censorship, the world will come out good and black. The romantic democrats of the early nine-teenth century would never have dreamed that a hundred and fifty years later the police spy and the censor would still be standing guard over our minds. To live in Eastern Europe is like reading about ourselves in a nineteenth-century Russian novel.

Ever since I was five years old I have known that there are things it is dangerous to talk about in front of strangers. Now I am approaching fifty, and I am still beset by a hateful anxiety that there may be trouble over something I have written. I have no more passionate desire for my young friends than that they dispel the censorship around them, wherever and however they can, so that at fifty they won't have to put up with this wretched feeling, unworthy of a grown man. May they develop an anticensorship sensibility; may they stop regarding silence as normal; and if they compromise, may they hold out separately for each single word, because generosity toward the censor is simply piecemeal self-abandonment.

I experienced the two historic wars that saw first German and then Russian troops occupy our country and gave various Hungarians an opportunity to settle accounts with other Hungarians. We haven't just been occupied ever since, we have been *possessed* in both senses of the word. I feel that my countrymen and I are sick from the restraints imposed upon us, which prevent us either individually or jointly from doing what we think best.

I recognize my Eastern European readers in myself, including those who would like to believe that they have nothing to do with politics or with the kind of culture that has developed in our area. I know what goes on inside me when I try to live with it, or against it, or without it. Not one of us can escape from the constant provocation of lack of freedom. Those who don't notice the effect that lack has on them are the sickest of all.

Press censorship is only one part of the Censorship, that officious, well-meaning spirit of disapproval, that pedagogical demand that we be like the grumbling but obedient majority, that we respond to the sane and friendly expectation that we will come to our senses, because anyone who is against the Censorship must have a screw loose somewhere—must be the victim of some congenital abnormality, some pathological spell, unable as he is to take for granted what exists, determined to see reality as it is as ridiculous. Come out with what is deepest in you, defend yourselves against the world, don't let anything outside your control get a grip on you. Study it with paranoid watchfulness.

That alleged and notorious reality which is there even when you are not, that reality before which you are very little (existing at all only by its leave)—try to look it in the eye. Whether its name is matter or communism or God, say to it with your jaw trembling: you are you, but I'm still me. I resist your power to possess. I don't want to acknowledge that you do with me whatever you like. You can't butter your bread with me, I don't belong to you. I am not a realist, I am not a moderate, I am not a conservative, even though I am realistic, moderate, and conservative. I refuse to be called to order according to the prescribed penalties. I say a considered but firm "no." I try to sense the secret logic hidden in my instincts that tells me to say "yes" sometimes and at other times "no." I am trying to slow the onrush of schizophrenia into the charmed circle of a sound mind. Of course I am small before the great, weak before the powerful, cowardly before the violent, wavering before the aggressive, expendable before It, which is so vast and durable that I sometimes think it is immortal. I don't turn the other cheek to it, I don't shoot at it with a slingshot; I look, and then I collect my words.

Csobánka-Budapest, 1982